# Home Econo
# Teacher's Guide

## CONTENTS

**Author:** **Marcia Parker, M.Ed.**
Editor: Alan Christopherson, M.S.

Alpha Omega Publications®

804 N. 2nd Ave. E., Rock Rapids, IA 51246-1759
© MM by Alpha Omega Publications, Inc.   All rights reserved.
LIFEPAC is a registered trademark of Alpha Omega Publications, Inc.

# OVERVIEW

# Home Economics

## Curriculum Overview

## LIFEPAC 1

**CHRISTIAN CHARACTER AND APPEARANCE**

INNER BEAUTY

A. Character Qualities

B. Biblical Principles vs. Personal Preferences

C. Personal Strengths and Weaknesses

PHYSICAL BEAUTY

A. Health

B. Nutrition and Exercise

C. Hygiene

D. Grooming

E. Posture

BEHAVIORAL BEAUTY

A. Actions

B. Communications

## LIFEPAC 2

**WHAT'S COOKIN'?**

GETTING ACQUAINTED WITH THE KITCHEN

A. Types of Utensils

B. Large Kitchen Equipment

C. Small Kitchen Appliances

D. Utensils

E. Safety in the Kitchen

RECIPES

A. What to look for in a good recipe

B. Recipe Ingredients

MEAL MANAGEMENT

A. Food Budget

B. Supermarket Smarts

C. Reading Labels

D. Food Storage

## LIFEPAC 3

**LET'S EAT**

NUTRITION

A. Nutrients

B. Food Pyramid

C. Heart Healthy Eating and Special Diets

FOOD PREPARATION

A. Cooking

B. Baking

MEAL PLANNING

A. Menus

B. Making a Grocery List

FOOD SERVICE

A. Styles of Table Service

B. Table Settings

C. Table Waiting

## LIFEPAC 4

**THE CLOTHES YOU WEAR**

FASHION

A. The Purpose of Clothing

B. Fashion Knowledge

C. Wardrobe Inventory

DESIGN AND APPEARANCE

A. Principles and Elements of Design

B. Garment Styles and Parts

C. Clothes for You

TEXTILES AND FABRICS

A. Natural Fibers

B. Manmade Fibers

CARE OF CLOTHES

A. Mending

B. Laundering

## LIFEPAC 5

THE CLOTHES YOU SEW

### SEWING EQUIPMENT AND SAFETY

A. Small Tools
B. Sewing Machine
C. Safety

### BASIC SEWING

A. Hand Stitches
B. Machine Stitches
C. Seams and Seam Finishes
D. Darts, Tucks, Pleats, Gathering and Facings
E. Closures

### SELECTING PATTERN, FABRIC AND NOTIONS

A. Fit
B. The Language of Patterns
C. Pattern
D. Fabric
E. Fabric Preparation
F. Notions

### LAYOUT, CUTTING, MARKING AND PRESSING

A. Layout
B. Cutting
C. Marking
D. Pressing

### SEWING PROJECT

A. Construction Checklist
B. Sewing Evaluation Form

## LIFEPAC 6

INTERIOR DECORATING

### A BRIEF HISTORY OF INTERIOR DESIGN

A. Continental Design
B. English Design
C. Traditional American Design
D. Twentieth Century Design

### INTRODUCTION TO DESIGN AND DECORATION

A. Elements and Principles of Design
B. Practical Techniques of Interior Design

### SPECIFIC TREATMENTS

A. Furniture
B. Floor Coverings
C. Wall Treatments
D. Window Treatments
E. Lighting

### VISUAL ENRICHMENT

A. Two-dimensional Objects
B. Three-dimensional Objects

### SEWING FOR THE HOME

A. A Brief Overview
B. Pillow Project

## LIFEPAC 7

YOUR HOME AND YOU

### HOSPITALITY

A. Planning to Entertain
B. Types of Entertainment
C. Overnight Guests

### ETIQUETTE

A. Table Etiquette and Conversation
B. Travel Etiquette
C. Dating Etiquette

### HOME MANAGEMENT

A. Household Maintenance
B. Auto Maintenance

## LIFEPAC 8

**FINANCIAL FREEDOM**

GETTING A JOB
  A. The Application Form
  B. The Résumé
  C. The Interview

PERSONAL FINANCE
  A. Personal Recordkeeping
  B. Personal Banking and Investments
  C. Personal Budgeting
  D. Credit Records
  E. Insurance
  F. Income Tax

LEGAL MATTERS FORMS AND CONTRACTS
  A. Bills of Sale
  B. Wills, Living Wills, Durable Power of Attorney
  C. Lease Agreements
  D. Purchasing and Owning a Car

## LIFEPAC 9

**CHILD DEVELOPMENT AND CARE**

AGES AND STAGES
  A. Physical (stature)
  B. Intellect (wisdom)
  C. Social (favor with man)
  D. Spiritual (favor with God)

CARE OF CHILDREN
  A. Basic Baby Care
  B. Creative Child Care
  C. Activities

SAFETY AND FIRST AID
  A. Prevention
  B. Problems
  C. Three Common Childhood Diseases

THE BUSINESS OF BABYSITTING
  A. Characteristics of a Dependable Baby-sitter
  B. Essential Business Practices
  C. Information You Need
  D. Baby-sitters Checklist

## LIFEPAC 10

**RELATIONSHIPS**

AT HOME
  A. Parents
  B. Siblings
  C. Grandparents

AT SCHOOL AND WORK
  A. Peers/Friends
  B. Teachers
  C. Boss and Co-workers

AT CHURCH
  A. The Church's Responsibility to the Family
  B. The Family's Responsibility to the Church

AT SOCIAL EVENTS
  A. Public Performances
  B. Sports Events
  C. Parties

CHOOSING THE RIGHT MATE
  A. What are You Looking For?
  B. Dating
    1. Going Out
    2. Breaking Up
    3. Sexuality
  C. Marriage
  D. Parental Involvement
  E. God's Involvement

LIFEPAC

M
A
N
A
G
E
M
E
N
T

## STRUCTURE OF THE LIFEPAC CURRICULUM

The LIFEPAC curriculum is conveniently structured to provide one teacher handbook containing teacher support material with answer keys and ten student worktexts for each subject at grade levels two through twelve. The worktext format of the LIFEPACs allows the student to read the textual information and complete workbook activities all in the same booklet. The easy to follow LIFEPAC numbering system lists the grade as the first number(s) and the last two digits as the number of the series. For example, the Language Arts LIFEPAC at the 6th grade level, 5th book in the series would be LA 605.

Each LIFEPAC is divided into 3 to 5 sections and begins with an introduction or overview of the booklet as well as a series of specific learning objectives to give a purpose to the study of the LIFEPAC. The introduction and objectives are followed by a vocabulary section which may be found at the beginning of each section at the lower levels, at the beginning of the LIFEPAC in the middle grades, or in the glossary at the high school level. Vocabulary words are used to develop word recognition and should not be confused with the spelling words introduced later in the LIFEPAC. The student should learn all vocabulary words before working the LIFEPAC sections to improve comprehension, retention and reading skills.

Each activity or written assignment has a number for easy identification, such as 1.1. The first number corresponds to the LIFEPAC section and the number to the right of the decimal is the number of the activity.

Adult checkpoints, which are essential to maintain quality learning, are found at various locations throughout the LIFEPAC. The teacher should check 1) neatness of work and penmanship, 2) quality of understanding (tested with a short oral quiz), 3) thoroughness of answers (complete sentences and paragraphs, correct spelling, etc.), 4) completion of activities (no blank spaces), and 5) accuracy of answers as compared to the answer key (all answers correct).

The self test questions are also number coded for easy reference. For example, 2.015 means that this is the 15th question in the self test of Section II. The first number corresponds to the LIFEPAC section, the zero indicates that it is a self test question, and the number to the right of the zero the question number.

The LIFEPAC test is packaged at the centerfold of each LIFEPAC. It should be removed and put aside before giving the booklet to the student for study.

Answer and test keys have the same numbering system as the LIFEPACs and appear at the back of this handbook. The student may be given access to the answer keys (not the test keys) under teacher supervision so that he can score his own work.

A thorough study of the Curriculum Overview by the teacher before instruction begins is essential to the success of the student. The teacher should become familiar with expected skill mastery and understand how these grade level skills fit into the overall skill development of the curriculum. The teacher should also preview the objectives that appear at the beginning of each LIFEPAC for additional preparation and planning.

## TEST SCORING and GRADING

Answer keys and test keys give examples of correct answers. They convey the idea, but the student may use many ways to express a correct answer. The teacher should check for the essence of the answer, not for the exact wording. Many questions are high level and require thinking and creativity on the part of the student. Each answer should be scored based on whether or not the main idea written by the student matches the model example. "Any Order" or "Either Order" in a key indicates that no particular order is necessary to be correct.

Most self tests and LIFEPAC tests at the lower elementary levels are scored at 1 point per question; however, the upper levels may have a point system awarding 2 to 5 points for various questions. Further, the total test points will vary; they may not always equal 100 points. They may be 78, 85, 100, 105, etc.

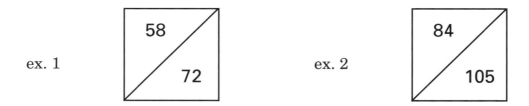

ex. 1     58 / 72       ex. 2     84 / 105

A score box similar to ex.1 above is located at the end of each self test and on the front of the LIFEPAC test. The bottom score, 72, represents the total number of points possible on the test. The upper score, 58, represents the number of points your student will need to receive an 80% or passing grade. If you wish to establish the exact percentage that your student has achieved, find the total points of his correct answers and divide it by the bottom number (in this case 72.) For example, if your student has a point total of 65, divide 65 by 72 for a grade of 90%. Referring to ex. 2, on a test with a total of 105 possible points, the student would have to receive a minimum of 84 correct points for an 80% or passing grade. If your student has received 93 points, simply divide the 93 by 105 for a percentage grade of 89%. Students who receive a score below 80% should review the LIFEPAC and retest using the appropriate Alternate Test found in the Teacher's Guide.

The following is a guideline to assign letter grades for completed LIFEPACs based on a maximum total score of 100 points.

LIFEPAC Test  =  60% of the Total Score (or percent grade)
Self Test      =  25% of the Total Score (average percent of self tests)
Reports       =  10% or 10* points per LIFEPAC
Oral Work    =  5% or 5* points per LIFEPAC

*Determined by the teacher's subjective evaluation of the student's daily work.

Example:

| | | | | | | | |
|---|---|---|---|---|---|---|---|
| LIFEPAC Test Score | = | 92% | 92 | x | .60 | = | 55 points |
| Self Test Average | = | 90% | 90 | x | .25 | = | 23 points |
| Reports | | | | | | = | 8 points |
| Oral Work | | | | | | = | 4 points |

_____

TOTAL POINTS    =    90 points

Grade Scale based on point system:

| | | | | |
|---|---|---|---|---|
| 100 | – | 94 | = | A |
| 93 | – | 86 | = | B |
| 85 | – | 77 | = | C |
| 76 | – | 70 | = | D |
| Below | | 70 | = | F |

## TEACHER HINTS and STUDYING TECHNIQUES

LIFEPAC Activities are written to check the level of understanding of the preceding text. The student may look back to the text as necessary to complete these activities; however, a student should never attempt to do the activities without reading (studying) the text first. Self tests and LIFEPAC tests are never open book tests.

Writing complete answers (paragraphs) to some questions is an integral part of the LIFEPAC Curriculum in all subjects. This builds communication and organization skills, increases understanding and retention of ideas, and helps enforce good penmanship. Complete sentences should be encouraged for this type of activity. Obviously, single words or phrases do not meet the intent of the activity, since multiple lines are given for the response.

Review is essential to student success. Time invested in review where review is suggested will be time saved in correcting errors later. Self tests, unlike the section activities, are closed book. This procedure helps to identify weaknesses before they become too great to overcome. Certain objectives from self tests are cumulative and test previous sections; therefore, good preparation for a self test must include all material studied up to that testing point.

The following procedure checklist has been found to be successful in developing good study habits in the LIFEPAC curriculum.

1. Read the introduction and Table of Contents.
2. Read the objectives.
3. Recite and study the entire vocabulary (glossary) list.
4. Study each section as follows:
    a. Read the introduction and study the section objectives.
    b. Read all the text for the entire section, but answer none of the activities.
    c. Return to the beginning of the section and memorize each vocabulary word and definition.
    d. Reread the section, complete the activities, check the answers with the answer key, correct all errors, and have the Adult check.
    e. Read the self test but do not answer the questions.
    f. Go to the beginning of the first section and reread the text and answers to the activities up to the self test you have not yet done.
    g. Answer the questions to the self test without looking back.
    h. Have the self test checked by the teacher.
    i. Correct the self test and have the teacher check the corrections.
    j. Repeat steps a–i for each section.

5. Use the SQ3R* method to prepare for the LIFEPAC test.
6. Take the LIFEPAC test as a closed book test.
7. LIFEPAC tests are administered and scored under direct teacher supervision. Students who receive scores below 80% should review the LIFEPAC using the SQ3R* study method and take the Alternate Test located in the Teacher Handbook. The final test grade may be the grade on the Alternate Test or an average of the grades from the original LIFEPAC test and the Alternate Test.

    *SQ3R: Scan the whole LIFEPAC.
            Question yourself on the objectives.
            Read the whole LIFEPAC again.
            Recite through an oral examination.
            Review weak areas.

## GOAL SETTING and SCHEDULES

Each school must develop its own schedule, because no single set of procedures will fit every situation. The following is an example of a daily schedule that includes the five LIFEPAC subjects as well as time slotted for special activities.

Possible Daily Schedule

| | | | |
|---|---|---|---|
| 8:15 | – | 8:25 | Pledges, prayer, songs, devotions, etc. |
| 8:25 | – | 9:10 | Bible |
| 9:10 | – | 9:55 | Language Arts |
| 9:55 | – | 10:15 | Recess (juice break) |
| 10:15 | – | 11:00 | Mathematics |
| 11:00 | – | 11:45 | Social Studies |
| 11:45 | – | 12:30 | Lunch, recess, quiet time |
| 12:30 | – | 1:15 | Science |
| 1:15 | – | | Drill, remedial work, enrichment* |

*Enrichment: Computer time, physical education, field trips, fun reading, games and puzzles, family business, hobbies, resource persons, guests, crafts, creative work, electives, music appreciation, projects.

Basically, two factors need to be considered when assigning work to a student in the LIFEPAC curriculum.

The first is time. An average of 45 minutes should be devoted to each subject, each day. Remember, this is only an average. Because of extenuating circumstances a student may spend only 15 minutes on a subject one day and the next day spend 90 minutes on the same subject.

The second factor is the number of pages to be worked in each subject. A single LIFEPAC is designed to take 3 to 4 weeks to complete. Allowing about 3-4 days for LIFEPAC introduction, review, and tests, the student has approximately 15 days to complete the LIFEPAC pages. Simply take the number of pages in the LIFEPAC, divide it by 15 and you will have the number of pages that must be completed on a daily basis to keep the student on schedule. For example, a LIFEPAC containing 45 pages will require 3 completed pages per day. Again, this is only an average. While working a 45 page LIFEPAC, the student may complete only 1 page the first day if the text has a lot of activities or reports, but go on to complete 5 pages the next day.

Long range planning requires some organization. Because the traditional school year originates in the early fall of one year and continues to late spring of the following year, a calendar should be devised that covers this period of time. Approximate beginning and completion dates can be noted on the calendar as well as special occasions such as holidays, vacations and birthdays. Since each LIFEPAC takes 3-4 weeks or eighteen days to complete, it should take about

180 school days to finish a set of ten LIFEPACs. Starting at the beginning school date, mark off eighteen school days on the calendar and that will become the targeted completion date for the first LIFEPAC. Continue marking the calendar until you have established dates for the remaining nine LIFEPACs making adjustments for previously noted holidays and vacations. If all five subjects are being used, the ten established target dates should be the same for the LIFEPACs in each subject.

## *FORMS*

The sample weekly lesson plan and student grading sheet forms are included in this section as teacher support materials and may be duplicated at the convenience of the teacher.

The student grading sheet is provided for those who desire to follow the suggested guidelines for assignment of letter grades found on page 3 of this section. The student's self test scores should be posted as percentage grades. When the LIFEPAC is completed the teacher should average the self test grades, multiply the average by .25 and post the points in the box marked self test points. The LIFEPAC percentage grade should be multiplied by .60 and posted. Next, the teacher should award and post points for written reports and oral work. A report may be any type of written work assigned to the student whether it is a LIFEPAC or additional learning activity. Oral work includes the student's ability to respond orally to questions which may or may not be related to LIFEPAC activities or any type of oral report assigned by the teacher. The points may then be totaled and a final grade entered along with the date that the LIFEPAC was completed.

The Student Record Book which was specifically designed for use with the Alpha Omega curriculum provides space to record weekly progress for one student over a nine week period as well as a place to post self test and LIFEPAC scores. The Student Record Books are available through the current Alpha Omega catalog; however, unlike the enclosed forms these books are not for duplication and should be purchased in sets of four to cover a full academic year.

# WEEKLY LESSON PLANNER

**Week of:**

| | Subject | Subject | Subject | Subject |
|---|---|---|---|---|
| **Monday** | | | | |
| **Tuesday** | | | | |
| **Wednesday** | | | | |
| **Thursday** | | | | |
| **Friday** | | | | |

# WEEKLY LESSON PLANNER

**Week of:**

| Subject | Subject | Subject | Subject |
|---|---|---|---|
| **Monday** | | | |

| Subject | Subject | Subject | Subject |
|---|---|---|---|
| **Tuesday** | | | |

| Subject | Subject | Subject | Subject |
|---|---|---|---|
| **Wednesday** | | | |

| Subject | Subject | Subject | Subject |
|---|---|---|---|
| **Thursday** | | | |

| Subject | Subject | Subject | Subject |
|---|---|---|---|
| **Friday** | | | |

Student Name _____     Year _____

## Bible

| LP # | Self Test Scores by Sections 1 | 2 | 3 | 4 | 5 | Self Test Points | LIFEPAC Test | Oral Points | Report Points | Final Grade | Date |
|------|------|------|------|------|------|------|------|------|------|------|------|
| 01 | | | | | | | | | | | |
| 02 | | | | | | | | | | | |
| 03 | | | | | | | | | | | |
| 04 | | | | | | | | | | | |
| 05 | | | | | | | | | | | |
| 06 | | | | | | | | | | | |
| 07 | | | | | | | | | | | |
| 08 | | | | | | | | | | | |
| 09 | | | | | | | | | | | |
| 10 | | | | | | | | | | | |

## History & Geography

| LP # | Self Test Scores by Sections 1 | 2 | 3 | 4 | 5 | Self Test Points | LIFEPAC Test | Oral Points | Report Points | Final Grade | Date |
|------|------|------|------|------|------|------|------|------|------|------|------|
| 01 | | | | | | | | | | | |
| 02 | | | | | | | | | | | |
| 03 | | | | | | | | | | | |
| 04 | | | | | | | | | | | |
| 05 | | | | | | | | | | | |
| 06 | | | | | | | | | | | |
| 07 | | | | | | | | | | | |
| 08 | | | | | | | | | | | |
| 09 | | | | | | | | | | | |
| 10 | | | | | | | | | | | |

## Language Arts

| LP # | Self Test Scores by Sections 1 | 2 | 3 | 4 | 5 | Self Test Points | LIFEPAC Test | Oral Points | Report Points | Final Grade | Date |
|------|------|------|------|------|------|------|------|------|------|------|------|
| 01 | | | | | | | | | | | |
| 02 | | | | | | | | | | | |
| 03 | | | | | | | | | | | |
| 04 | | | | | | | | | | | |
| 05 | | | | | | | | | | | |
| 06 | | | | | | | | | | | |
| 07 | | | | | | | | | | | |
| 08 | | | | | | | | | | | |
| 09 | | | | | | | | | | | |
| 10 | | | | | | | | | | | |

Student Name _____     Year _____

## Mathematics

| LP # | Self Test Scores by Sections 1 | 2 | 3 | 4 | 5 | Self Test Points | LIFEPAC Test | Oral Points | Report Points | Final Grade | Date |
|------|---|---|---|---|---|---|---|---|---|---|---|
| 01 | | | | | | | | | | | |
| 02 | | | | | | | | | | | |
| 03 | | | | | | | | | | | |
| 04 | | | | | | | | | | | |
| 05 | | | | | | | | | | | |
| 06 | | | | | | | | | | | |
| 07 | | | | | | | | | | | |
| 08 | | | | | | | | | | | |
| 09 | | | | | | | | | | | |
| 10 | | | | | | | | | | | |

## Science

| LP # | Self Test Scores by Sections 1 | 2 | 3 | 4 | 5 | Self Test Points | LIFEPAC Test | Oral Points | Report Points | Final Grade | Date |
|------|---|---|---|---|---|---|---|---|---|---|---|
| 01 | | | | | | | | | | | |
| 02 | | | | | | | | | | | |
| 03 | | | | | | | | | | | |
| 04 | | | | | | | | | | | |
| 05 | | | | | | | | | | | |
| 06 | | | | | | | | | | | |
| 07 | | | | | | | | | | | |
| 08 | | | | | | | | | | | |
| 09 | | | | | | | | | | | |
| 10 | | | | | | | | | | | |

## Spelling/Electives

| LP # | Self Test Scores by Sections 1 | 2 | 3 | 4 | 5 | Self Test Points | LIFEPAC Test | Oral Points | Report Points | Final Grade | Date |
|------|---|---|---|---|---|---|---|---|---|---|---|
| 01 | | | | | | | | | | | |
| 02 | | | | | | | | | | | |
| 03 | | | | | | | | | | | |
| 04 | | | | | | | | | | | |
| 05 | | | | | | | | | | | |
| 06 | | | | | | | | | | | |
| 07 | | | | | | | | | | | |
| 08 | | | | | | | | | | | |
| 09 | | | | | | | | | | | |
| 10 | | | | | | | | | | | |

## INSTRUCTION FOR HOME ECONOMICS

The LIFEPAC curriculum from grades two through twelve is structured so that the daily instructional material is written directly into the LIFEPACs. The student is encouraged to read and follow this instructional material in order to develop independent study habits. The teacher should introduce the LIFEPAC to the student, set a required completion schedule, complete Adult checks, be available for questions regarding both content and procedures, administer and grade tests, and develop additional learning activities as desired. Teachers working with several students may schedule their time so that students are assigned to a quiet work activity when it is necessary to spend instructional time with one particular student.

The Teacher Notes section of the handbook lists the required or suggested materials for the LIFEPACs and provides additional learning activities for the students. The materials section refers only to LIFEPAC materials and does not include materials which may be needed for the additional activities. Additional learning activities provide a change from the daily school routine, encourage the student's interest in learning, and may be used as a reward for good study habits.

**Materials needed for LIFEPAC 1**

Required:

Hand cream
Cotton balls
Nail file
Cuticle cream
Cuticle remover
Nail brush
Orange stick
Buffing cream
Nail buffer

Suggested:

Nail polish remover
Nail base coat
Nail polish
Nail top coat

**ADDITIONAL LEARNING ACTIVITIES:**

**Section I** Inner Beauty

1. Girls: Read the book *Patterns from Proverbs 31,* by Sharon Rhoades, filling in the work book as you go.

2. Boys: Choose a character from the Bible, such as Paul and do a character study of his life. List the character qualities that you find such as faithful.

3. Look up on the Internet, the Myers-Briggs type Indicator. It is a test to find out your personality type. Take this test for fun. There are other personality tests available as well.

**Section II** Physical Beauty

1. Go to a hair salon and have your hair styled. Have a manicure or pedicure. If you can locate a beauty school near your home, you will find their prices very reasonable for this fun outing. Or, have a friend over and give each other manicures or pedicures.

2. After determining what skin type you are, go through the steps for facial cleansing. Even guys can have fun experiencing the use of a facial mask. A fun thing to do for girls is to go to a department store cosmetic counter and ask for a free facial and makeup demonstration.

3. If you are really struggling with diet a suggested book that is recommended by many doctors, is *Choose to Lose,* by Dr. Ron Goor and Nancy Goor. The book contains the tools and knowledge to make dietary changes that will keep you healthy for a lifetime. It contains food tables that give the total calories, saturated fat calories, and fat calories for hundreds of food items, including commercial products, fast foods, and restaurant choices. It provides information about the importance of carbohydrates and fiber in the diet. This book not only points out the don'ts, but it also provides the answers to dietary questions and solutions to problems.

**Section III** Behavioral Beauty

1. Study the attributes of being a lady or gentleman (see the LIFEPAC) and list those you think that you possess. Have a friend make a list of the attributes that they think you have. Compare lists and determine what you need to do to improve your behavior so that you will become more of a lady or gentleman.

2. Practice introductions with a friend or teacher. Use a variety of ages, stations, and sexes.

**Materials needed for LIFEPAC 2**

Required:

A variety of recipe books or files.

Suggested:

A fully equipped kitchen facility either at school or at home.
Access to various food product labels.
A variety of markets for comparison.

## ADDITIONAL LEARNING ACTIVITIES:

**Section I** Getting Acquainted with the Kitchen

1. Visit a Home Improvement type store and compare the various kitchen styles of cabinets, flooring, lighting and appliances.

**Section II** Recipes

1. Begin your own recipe file by collecting family favorites from all of your close relatives. Put them in a recipe file or purchase a blank recipe book.

2. Get the recipes for those special occasions and holidays.

**Section III** Meal Management

1. Visit a grocery store, compare prices, brands, convenience of store layouts.

2. Visit a farmer's market. It will be fun. Write a short paragraph sharing about this unique experience. How does the farmer's market compare with your regular super market?

**Materials needed for LIFEPAC 3**

Required:

Book: *Nutritive Value of Foods*

Various recipe books or files

Sauce pans with lids of various sizes, stirring spoons, cutting knives, cutting board, serving salad bowl, stew pot or crock pot, rolling pin, mixing bowls, measuring spoons and cups, cookie and various other kitchen appliances and utensils as required by individual recipes.

Recipes and ingredients for oatmeal or cream of wheat, fresh broccoli, ambrosia or fresh fruit salad, baked macaroni and cheese, vegetable and beef stew, a favorite soup or salad, cookie, cake, pie and yeast bread.

Access to a supermarket.

Supplies for one place setting: dinner plate, bread plate with knife, dinner knife, spoon, soup spoon, dinner fork, salad fork, dessert fork and spoon, napkin, water glass, beverage glass, and cup and saucer.

Suggested:

Fancy Cover Mat
Service Plate
Liner Plates
Place settings for the whole family.
A fully equipped kitchen facility either at school or at home.

**ADDITIONAL LEARNING ACTIVITIES:**

**Section I** Nutrition

1. Research and write a report on one of the special dietary needs mentioned in the reading such as diabetes or anorexia nervosa.

**Section II** Food Preparation

1. Bake a cake for a special occasion. Decorate it using special decorating tubes and tips. Incorporate special edges, flowers with leaves (rosettes, daisies, carnations) piping, writing, etc. Be very creative and have fun. *This will require the purchase of at least a minimal decorating set. Wilton's makes a variety of sizes of sets along with instructions. Also it is fun to bake in novelty cake pans such as a tennis shoe, T-shirt, or cartoon character pans. These are a little expensive, however.

**Section III** Meal Planning

1. Plan, prepare, and serve a special dinner for your school principal and/or pastor along with their wives, or a group of four or more adult couples. This can be a lot of fun and a great experience. Prepare several courses: appetizer, salad/soup, main course (something fancy like Cornish Hens), dessert, and demitasse. Be sure to use garnish. Select a formal style of service and set the table accordingly. This is a great class project.

2. Collect and file several menus from different special occasions such as Thanksgiving, Christmas Eve, Christmas Day, and New Year's Eve. Family traditions handed down are a great gift for future generations.

**Section IV** Food Service

1. One of the simplest ways of making an occasion out of a meal is to fold the napkins in clever ways. Go to the library and check out several books on napkinology or napkin folding. Experiment folding napkins different ways. It will delight your guests to see how creative and festive you are able to make your table look with a few simple napkin folds. You will need several starched linen napkins for practice.

**Napkinology Tips**

1. It is best to experiment new and difficult folds on newer napkins. They have more body than heavily laundered napkins.

2. Napkins should be starched for good support and a crisp look. It is best to press napkins when slightly damp for a fresh, firm look.

3. Square napkins are easier to work with than rectangular ones.

4. Patterned fabrics may need a little more practice and patience since some prints are only on one side.

5. REMEMBER–It is easier to fold napkins than it may first appear! Don't be afraid to experiment with some new and challenging ideas.

**Materials needed for LIFEPAC 4**

Required:

Magazines, fashion types and
catalogs such as Sears® or J.C. Penney's®
are best
Pencil, colored pencils or crayons
Basic Mending Kit: see list of
supplies in Section IV

Container to keep supplies in
3-ring binder or loose-leaf notebook
Plain white paper for notebook
Glue
Material remnants
Double-faced mending tape
Fusible web

**ADDITIONAL LEARNING ACTIVITIES:**

**Section I** Fashion

1. Write a 3 page (typewritten) report on the history of fashion.

2. You are to research a fashion designer. You may choose the designer you wish to research from the following list. Write a 2-3 page (type written) report. Try to include pictures. Suggested sources, found at most public libraries: *Who's Who in Fashion, Eleanor Lamberts World of Fashion, The Fashion Makers,* Fashion Magazines, *Readers Guide to Periodicals.*

Adrian, Gilbert (1903–59). American.

Balenciaga, Cristóbal (1895–1972). Spanish.

Burrows, Stephen (born 1943). American.

Chanel, Coco (1883–1971).

Courrèges, André (born 1923). French.

Dior, Christian (1905–57). French.

Ellis, Perry (1940–86). American.

Gernreich, Rudi (1922–85). Austrian-American.

Kenzo (born 1939). Japanese.

Klein, Anne (1923–74). American.

Lauren, Ralph (born 1939). American.

McCardell, Claire (1905–58). American.

Norell, Norman (1900–72). American.

Rabanne, Paco (born 1934). Spanish.

Rhodes, Zandra (born 1940). British.

Saint Laurent, Yves (born 1936). French.

Schiaparelli, Elsa (1896–1973). Italian-French.

**Section II** Design and Appearance

1. Go on a shopping adventure. Find the color, line, texture, for your body by trying on a variety of clothes with different styles and fabrics. Look in the mirror and take note of what looks good and what does not compliment your figure.

2. Be color draped. This can be expensive unless you know someone who is knowledgeable in color draping and is willing to demonstrate to the class or do a personal draping of the student for free. Color draping kits are also available to purchase. Color draping is the process of determining whether you are a winter, spring, summer, or fall by choosing the colors that complement your skin tones, hair and eye color.

**Section III** Textiles and Fabrics

1. Field trip to a fabric store. This activity will have a two-fold purpose. First, the student(s) will become familiar with the layout of a sewing store so that when they must make a purchase of a pattern, fabric and notions for their sewing project in LIFEPAC 5 they will be more at ease. Second, the student will become more acquainted with the different types of fabrics available for their sewing projects.

At the store, the student(s) should find fabric examples that contain each of the four natural fibers and as many of the man-made fibers as possible. Have them make a list.

It would be good also to show them how to check for laundering instructions on the ends of bolts and how to purchase fabric.

This could also be an opportunity for the student(s) to purchase their basic mending kit as listed in Section 4 of the LIFEPAC. At least show the students the different areas of the store, like notions, fabrics, sewing supplies, etc.

**Section IV**  Care of Clothes

1. Take several different types of fabric remnants and stain them with various stains; then try to remove the stains using the methods in the chart found in the LIFEPAC. (Various cleaning supplies such as soap, cleaning fluid, petroleum jelly, cornstarch or talc, white blotting paper, milk, nail-polish remover, and turpentine will be needed.)

2. Mend and clean the clothes in your own closet.

**Materials needed for LIFEPAC 5**

Required:

Basic mending kit from LIFEPAC 4
Dressmaker sewing shears
Sewing Machine
Sewing machine needle
Thread for sewing skills practice
Bobbin
Tracing wheel and tracing paper
Approximately 20 - 6″ square fabric pieces
1 - 8″ square fabric piece
1 - 9″ x 6″ fabric piece
1 - 6″ zipper
Sewing project pattern, fabric and notions

Suggested Class Policies for Sewing Unit: These are rules used for a classroom situation but can be modified for any sewing instruction class.

1. Be in your seat when the bell rings.

2. There is to be no LOUD talking in the clothing lab during class time. If noise gets out of hand this rule will be changed to NO TALKING at all.

3. No one may borrow another student's equipment.

4. Your name must be on each piece of your personal sewing equipment and on each pattern piece.

5. Any misplaced items should be put in a "lost and found" box.

6. Keep your equipment box clean and organized at all times. There will be surprise checks.

7. Department equipment must be put in the proper place after every class.

8. Irons must be clean at all times and should be turned off when they are not in use. Pressing equipment must be put away at the end of each class hour.

9. Begin to clean up the last five minutes of class. No one should leave before they are dismissed.

10. Nothing can be left on the tables or counters after class is dismissed.

11. Your bobbins should be removed at the end of the hour.

12. All machine work on projects and files must be done in class. Hand work and pressing may be done at home.

Suggested:

Several patterns and envelopes for demonstration and reference.

Old pattern books from cloth stores for classroom use.

1 zipper for optional fly front application skill activity

**ADDITIONAL LEARNING ACTIVITIES:**

**Section I** Sewing Equipment and Safety

1. Teacher should go over class policies for the sewing unit with students.

2. Instructor bring examples of each of the different types of sewing needles listed in the chart and demonstrate their use on the appropriate fabrics. Allow students to experience using these needles as well.

**Section II** Basic Sewing

1. After the student has demonstrated skill in naming the parts of the sewing machine, have him/her repeat the activity and this time explain the function of each part.

2. Student should inspect the clothes in their closets, looking for any mending or alteration needs. Students should then mend or alter clothes accordingly.

3. Practice making the different types of pleats listed in the text: side (knife) pleats, box pleats, inverted pleats, accordion pleats, and pleats with a separate underlay. Use any sewing guide book for instructions.

**Section III** Selecting Pattern, Fabric and Notions.

1. Practice measuring a variety of people to determine figure/body type and pattern size. Make and fill out a similar chart as the one given in LIFEPAC 5. Look in a pattern book, and select some styles that would compliment each person that you measure.

2. Compare pattern envelopes, guide sheets, symbols, etc. from various pattern companies to become familiar with their likes and differences. These will be subtle, but it is good to be prepared ahead of time. You may find some pattern instructions are more user friendly than others.

**Section IV** Layout, Cutting, Marking and Pressing

1. Use the extra patterns provided in the classroom to practice different layout schematics.

**Section V** Sewing Project

1. Find a partner and check each other's project layouts for accuracy before having the instructor check your work.

2. Continue with this same partner and check one another's work as your sewing projects progress.

**Materials needed for LIFEPAC 6**

Required:

3-ring binder notebook
White paper, 8 1/2″ x 11″
Magazines, furniture catalogs, & furniture sales ads
Markers or crayons, pencils, eraser, ruler, scissors
Tape measure
Graph paper 8 1/2″ x 11″
Pkg. of 3″ x 5″ cards for assignment

Tracing paper 8 1/2″ x 11″
Selected samples and/or pictures of floor coverings, wall coverings, window treatments, light fixtures, bedroom furniture and furnishings, and bedroom accessories for visual enrichment.

Suggested:

Plastic zipper notebook pencil bag
T-square or triangle
Envelope or plastic zippered bags

* Students will need to develop an interior design notebook similar to their "Sewing Skills Notebook." Again I suggest a loose-leaf notebook with plain white paper to attach samples, pictures and descriptions. Each page should be labeled and each item on the page should be identified.

## ADDITIONAL LEARNING ACTIVITIES

**Section I**  A Brief History of Interior Design

1.  Write a report on a furniture designer; include information about the time period in which he lived, characteristics of his particular design, examples of his works and how his design influenced American furniture design.

2.  Slides and Book: There is available through the Phoenix Art Museum, slide pictures of a special room in the museum. This room exhibits the Thorne Miniature Rooms created from the personal collection of miniature objects belonging to Narcissa Thorne. Many of the Thorne Rooms are exact replicas of rooms in existing great houses in the United States and abroad. Each room depicts the architecture and interior design of their periods and countries. Both the slides and book show the sixteen Miniature Rooms that are a permanent exhibit of the Phoenix Art Museum in memorial to Marie B. Thorne, 1962. Both the book and the slides are available for purchase through the Gift Shop at the museum: Phoenix Art Museum, Phoenix, AZ. 1625 N. Central Ave., Phoenix, AZ 85004 602-257-1222. (www.phxart.org and email: info@phxart.org.)

Ideas for magazines: *Better Homes and Gardens* and *Martha Stewart's Living,* etc.
Ideas for furniture: *Sears®, J.C. Penney's®, Montgomery Ward®, Ethan Allen® Home Interiors* and *Rob and Stucky®.*

3.  Field Trip: There are a number of places where American antique furniture can viewed. Below is a list of some of the many institutions available.

**East Coast:**

Albany Institute of History and Art, Albany, NY.
Baltimore Museum of Art, Baltimore, MD
Bascobel Restoration, Garrison, NY
Brooklyn Museum, Brooklyn, NY
Concord Antiquarian Museum, Concord, MA
Connecticut Historical Society, Hartford, CT
Craftsman Farms, Morris Plains, NJ
Daughters of the American Revolution Museum, Washington, DC
Essex Institute, Salem, MA
Metropolitan Museum of Art, New York City, NY
Museum of Fine Arts, Boston, MA
Newport Historical Society, Newport, RI
Old Sturbridge Village, Sturbridge, MA
Philadelphia Museum of Art, Philadelphia, PA
Pilgrim Hall (Plymouth Village), Plymouth, MA

Rhode Island School of Design, Museum of Art, Providence, RI
Strawberry Banke, Portsmouth, NH
Wadsworth Atheneum, Hartford, CT
Yale University Art Gallery, Mabel Brady Garvan and Related Collections, New Haven, CT

**South:**

Colonial Williamsburg, Williamsburg, VA
Grove Park Inn, Ashville, NC
High Museum of Art, Atlanta, GA
Historic Charleston Foundation, Charleston, SC
Museum of Early Southern Decorative Arts, Winston-Salem, NC

**Midwest:**

Art Institute of Chicago, IL
Cincinnati Art Museum, Cincinnati, OH
Frank Lloyd Wright Home, Oak Park, IL
Henry Ford Museum and Greenfield Village, Dearborn, MI
Missouri Historical Society, St. Louis, MO
Museum of Fine Arts, Bayou Bend Collection , Houston, TX
The St. Louis Art Museum, St. Louis, MO

**West:**

Fine Arts Museum of San Francisco, San Francisco, CA
Gamble House, Pasadena, CA
Lost Angeles County Museum of Art, Los Angeles, CA

    4. Field Trip: taking a field trip to an antique store and identifying period pieces of furniture could be a good learning experience. If the "Antique Road Show" is in your area, it could be fun to visit as well.

**Section II** Introduction to Design and Decoration

    1. Draw a floor plan for another room in your house. Find templates for the existing furniture and design two different arrangements.

**Section III** Specific Treatments and **IV** Visual Enrichment

    1. Select a room other than your bedroom. Through rearranging furniture, changing accessories (visual enrichment) and by using personal touches, see if you can alter the "spirit" of the room. This should be a cost-free project. Be creative.

**Section V** Sewing for the Home

    1. Complete a hand-made craft item for your bedroom, keeping in mind the theme and color scheme. Suggestions: cross stitch, embroidery a linen for on top of dresser, candlewick a decorative pillow, silk-floral arrangement, model airplane or ship, make wood baseball hat holder, make wooden shelf for knickknacks, paint a ceramic figurine or knickknack. The list of possibilities never ends.

**Materials needed for LIFEPAC 7**

Required:

Paper for making invitations and
decorations (construction, typing,
parchment, etc.)
Scissors, crayons, markers
Various cookbooks for menu planning
Hose with spray nozzle
Bucket, sponge, rags, newspaper
Vacuum
Leather or vinyl cleaner
Window cleaner

Suggested:

Thank-you notes or note cards
Chamois
Tire cleaner
Tar removing cleanser
Silicone spray
Stain remover
Car polish and/or wax
Car deodorizer
Party supplies

## ADDITIONAL LEARNING ACTIVITIES

**Section I** Hospitality

1. Design and create a floral arrangement or a centerpiece. Given below is a chart with several ideas.

2. Volunteer to help with a church banquet. The experience will be invaluable when you are put in charge of such a task in the future.

---

**Festive Centerpieces** *Without a Florist*

On a bamboo place mat, center a long brass or pottery planter filled with trailing ivy.

Place ivy in a large sea shell and put candles on either side of the shell.

Set out several pots of coleus or other interesting-looking plants.

Arrange "antique" toys from your childhood, such as trains, small trucks, or doll furniture, in the center of the table.

For New Year's Eve, make a clock by placing small stubby candles around a round glass or mirrored plate set on pine branches. Use a knife and fork for clock hands.

For Christmas, use a wreath of evergreens with tall red candles and pine cones in the center; or decorate the wreath of evergreens with candy canes and small red bows.

Place shiny Christmas tree balls inside a tall glass vase.

Float two peonies in a silver bowl.

Cut flowers from your garden and float one blossom each in glass tumblers of varying heights.

Place dried grass and seed pods in two small baskets and cluster three tall candles between.

Place a wreath of autumn leaves beneath a wooden bowl filled with green pears, green grapes and assorted unshelled nuts such as California walnuts and almonds.

Have ivy trailing from three tall candles.

Center a pumpkin on a wooden plate or tray with a cluster of oak leaves at the base.

Circle a pineapple with grapes, tangerines, pears and bananas.

Fill a basket with a large eggplant and tomatoes, or use other vegetables such as onions, turnips and potatoes.

Arrange a large spray of oak leaves and acorns with candles of varying heights nestled in it.

---

Lay sheaves of wheat down the center of the table and top them with grapes and apples.

On a wooden cutting board, arrange three or four interestingly shaped loaves of bread and several sheaves of wheat.

Fill apothecary jars with different unshelled nuts; place sprigs of bittersweet at the base.

Fill an old-fashioned coffee pot with greens.

Make an arrangement with your collection of sea shells.

Put tiny pots of herbs in a long French bread basket.

Arrange cactus plants in clay pots on a bright yellow place mat.

**Section II** Etiquette

1. In review, set up a formal dining place setting and explain when and how to use each appointment.

2. Practice having the gentleman seat the lady at a table. It takes both parties involved to make this a smooth action.

3. Take a friend on a date: call, ask, plan and pay. If you feel uncomfortable with asking a friend on a date, then ladies ask your Dad and gentlemen ask your Mom.

**Section III** Home Management

1. Help an elderly or disabled person by volunteering to clean his/her house.

2. Help an elderly or disabled person by volunteering to do some repairs around his/her house, such as painting, yard work, etc.

3. Help an elderly or disabled person by volunteering to clean his/her car.

4. Help an elderly or disabled person by volunteering to do some repairs on his/her car, such as check/change the oil, replace old windshield wipers, etc.

5. Change a tire on a car. Practice now will eliminate panic in an emergency.

**Materials needed for LIFEPAC 8**

Required:

Typing, computer or parchment paper
Ledger paper or lined paper

## ADDITIONAL LEARNING ACTIVITIES

**Section I** Getting a Job

1. Write a second resume, using one of the other two types of resumes. For example, if the resume you wrote for the LIFEPAC activity was a functional resume, then write either a chronological or combination type resume.

2. Set up an actual job interview. If you are a senior in high school, then you could substitute this actual job interview with a college entrance interview.

**Section II** Personal Finance

1. Visit a local bank to pick up information about its services. After you have reviewed this information, return to the bank; this time, see a customer service representative. Ask how the bank can help you with your finances.

2. If you have never balanced your check book register and reconciled the bank statement check register, then go through the steps with a parent or do this on your own account.

3. Research and decide what the best insurance options are for your family. You may have your parent(s) help you make your final decisions. Write a paper with your conclusions. Be sure to back your decisions up with facts and statistics.

4. Invest in the stock market. You have $20,000 with which to buy five stocks. Check the newspaper and Internet for a listing of stocks and their values. You have one month to see if you can increase your funds. You must trade at least three times within that time period. Keep careful records of your transactions: amounts, name of stocks, dates of purchases, and sales, etc.

5. Since this LIFEPAC will more than likely be studied in the spring. Take the opportunity to do your own taxes with parental guidance.

**Section III** Legal Matters, Forms, and Contracts

1. Go to a car dealership and ask them to explain the process of leasing a car. Since you are not really interested in buying a car at this time, tell the dealer that it is a school assignment but that you would appreciate him making it as realistic as possible. Are there any special rules concerning you as a minor in leasing a car? Go home and look at the cash flow chart you made in the LIFEPAC. Based on what the dealer has told you and what your cash flow chart reveals, do you have room in your budget to lease or buy a car? Don't forget to add those extra car expenses to your cash flow chart to get a truer picture of the total yearly expenses you will have to face.

2. Write a mock will for you or another family member. Type it up and sign it.

**Materials needed for LIFEPAC 9**

Required:

One cloth diaper
One set of diaper pins
One disposable diaper for each student
Real baby or life size doll
Pattern and supplies to make a stuffed toy
Supplies for children's book: paper,
crayons, magic markers, pencils, construction paper, old magazines, scissors,
glue, hole punch, yarn, brass fasteners
Finger paint supplies: flour, salt, water,
food coloring, sauce pan, spoon, finger
paint paper (banner or shelf paper would
do)
Playdough supplies: flour, salt, food coloring, water, bowl, plastic bag, wax paper

Suggested:

Smock
Old cookie cutters
Rolling pin
Toy hammer
Old garlic press

**ADDITIONAL LEARNING ACTIVITIES**

**Section I** Ages and Stages

1. Practice and demonstrate picking up and holding a baby.

2. Practice and demonstrate bathing and dressing a baby.

3. Shampoo your own hair and practice fun and crazy hairdos while the shampoo is still in your hair. This will help you see what fun it can be.

**Section II** Care of Children

1. Volunteer to work in your church nursery. Use the skills you have learned about the care of children such as changing diapers, picking up and holding both babies and young children, playing with children, etc.

2. Make a picture puzzle. You can make a wood puzzle by cutting a picture into puzzle shapes and tracing the outline of them onto a piece of plywood. Using a jigsaw, cut the puzzle pieces out of the plywood. Sand the wood so there are no rough edges. Carefully glue the picture pieces to the correct wood puzzle pieces. Using decoupage or epoxy glaze, cover each puzzle piece. There is also on the market at most craft stores already cut out cardboard puzzle pieces that you can glue the picture on or draw your own picture on. Children like to make their own pictures as well.

**Section III** Safety and First Aid

1. Put together your own first aid kit; it can be for baby-sitting purposes, camping, family car, etc.

2. If you have not already taken a First Aid class, do so. The American Red Cross offers classes in First Aid and CPR.

**Section IV** The Business of Babysitting

1. Make a baby-sitting kit; something you can take with you when you are to care for children whether it be in a home, at church, or camp. It should include: toys, games, puzzles, books, music tapes or CDs, portable recorder/tape/CD player, crayons or magic markers, plain pad of paper and/or coloring books, and a mini-first aid kit. Be creative and add whatever else you want.

2. Make a flyer to advertise in your neighborhood that you have a baby-sitting business.

**Materials needed for LIFEPAC 10**
   Required:                                                                Suggested:
      *Websters Dictionary* (preferably 1828 version)          None

**ADDITIONAL LEARNING ACTIVITIES:**

   **Section I** At Home

      1. Plan a family outing. Include parents, siblings and even grandparents.

      Activity: _____
      _____
      _____

      Who attended: _____
      _____
      _____

      Date _____ Time began _____ Time ended _____

      Did everyone seem to have a good time? _____

      Did you enjoy the experience? _____

      Did you learn any lessons about relationships? _____
      _____
      _____

      2. Tell of something you did as a child that made you very happy. Who were the other people
         involved? Tell how they were a direct or indirect influence on the event that made it a happy one.

   **Section II** At School and Work

      1. Study the three friends in the Book of Job. Either have a class debate or write a paper. Consider
         these questions. Were they true friends? Did they exemplify the qualities of true friendship?
         Why or why not? Would you want them for friends?

      2. Do a comparison study on the following three ladies of the Bible and write a one page paper on
         your findings. Each had a different work experience. What was it?

            Lydia - Acts 16:14, 15
            Priscilla - Acts 18:2, 3
            Mary (Mark's mother) - Acts 12:12f

(Teacher Help: Lydia was a single-working woman. Priscilla was a working wife, who made tents with her
husband. Mary presided over the running of a home.)

   **Section III** At Church

      1. After identifying the talents God has given to you and deciding where these fit into the min-
         istry of your church, volunteer to use one of these talents in some way: join a choir, decorate a
         bulletin board, assist in Sunday School class, minister in a nursing home, etc.

   **Section IV** At Social Events

      1. Prepare to be a kinder, more courteous, and gracious guest at a party: read a good, clean joke
         book, practice telling someone something funny that happened to you, practice introducing
         yourself and others.

      2. Give a gift to someone toward whom you have been bitter.

   **Section V** Choosing the Right Mate

      1. Make a list of the characteristic you think you need to have to be a good mate for someone else.
         Which ones do you think you have now? Which ones need more work?

# HOME ECONOMICS LIFEPAC 1 ALTERNATE TEST

**Name** _____

**Date** _____

**Score** _____

78 / 98

**Matching: Select the Christian quality that best fits the quotation** (each answer, 2 points).

1. _____ "I will behave with integrity."                          a.  knowledge

2. _____ "I will study scripture."                                b.  brotherly kindness

3. _____ "I will develop the ability to say, no."                 c.  patience

4. _____ "I will show concern for my fellow man."                d.  temperance

5. _____ "I will strive to be Christ-like."                       e.  godliness

6. _____ "I will cultivate forbearance in my relationships with others."   f.  charity

7. _____ "I will show love toward my Christian friends."          g.  virtue

**Determine if the following issues are (a) biblical principles or (b) personal preferences**
(each answer, 1 point).

8. _____ homosexuality

9. _____ long hair on men

10. _____ premarital sex

11. _____ women wearing slacks

12. _____ abortion

13. _____ dancing

**Matching** (each answer, 2 points).

14. _____ affects your heart                     a.  carbohydrates

15. _____ empty calories                         b.  salt

16. _____ affects your complexion                c.  eating too little

17. _____ affects your blood pressure            d.  sugar

18. _____ affects your energy level              e.  fat

**Answer the following** (each answer, 2 points).

19. How often should you shower?_____

20. What causes body odor? _____

21. What face shape lends itself to any hairstyle?_____

22. What is the focal point of the face?_____

23. What is the key to good posture? _____

24. What has replaced the "four food groups" concept? _____

25.    What is the key to proper nutrition?_____

26.    What are conversational "sweeteners"?_____

**Matching** (each answer, 2 points).

27.    _____ ability of muscles and joints to move freely.              a.  muscle strength

28.    _____ ability of heart and lungs to perform well during sustained exercise.    b.  muscle endurance

29.    _____ ability of muscles to work for a very long time.           c.  muscle flexibility

30.    _____ ability of muscles to do hard work.                        d.  aerobic endurance

**Define the following words** (each answer, 4 points).

31.    personality _____

       _____

32.    nutrients _____

       _____

33.    antiperspirant _____

       _____

34.    manicure _____

       _____

35.    carriage _____

       _____

36.    communication_____

       _____

**Short Answer. Select** *two* **of the following questions and answer as completely as you can using complete sentences** (each answer, 4 points).

37.    Select one of the following Biblical principles and explain what it teaches: Individuality; Self-government; Christian character; or Conscience, our most sacred property.

       _____

       _____

38.    Explain the relationship between health and hygiene.

       _____

       _____

39.    What does daily aerobic exercise do for your body?

       _____

       _____

40.    Outline the steps for skin care for dry skin.

       _____

       _____

41.    Introduce your mother to a friend.

       _____

       _____

# HOME ECONOMICS LIFEPAC 2 ALTERNATE TEST

**Name** _____

**Date** _____

**Score** _____

78 / 98

**Answer** *true* **or** *false* (each answer, 2 points).

1. _____ There should be 2 feet of work space on each side of the sink.

2. _____ In the ideal kitchen layout, the range should be between the sink and the refrigerator.

3. _____ A radiant oven circulates hot air around the oven cavity.

4. _____ Cabinets determine the "personality" of the kitchen.

5. _____ Roasting in a pan that is too big will cause juices to evaporate and burn.

6. _____ A soup pot is also known as a stock pot.

7. _____ You judge the quality of the knife blade by its sharpness and length.

8. _____ To smother a fire in an oven, open the door and use a fire extinguisher.

9. _____ There are four tablespoons in a half cup.

10. _____ You should always sift powdered sugar.

11. _____ Brown sugar should be packed down firmly for an accurate measurement.

12. _____ Sirloin steak has more protein than chuck steak.

13. _____ It is best to shop when you are not hungry.

14. _____ All frozen pizzas are made with real cheese.

15. _____ A Co-op is operated and owned by a group of people.

16. _____ Convenience stores are usually open 24 hours.

17. _____ The first item listed on the label of a product is most plentiful by percentage weight.

18. _____ The coolest section of the refrigerator is the vegetable drawer.

19. _____ Meat can be kept in the refrigerator 3-5 days.

20. _____ A rise in temperature stimulates microbiological activity.

21. _____ The chemical names for standard ingredients should be included on the label of products.

22. _____ "Fortified" signifies that a label lists additional nutrients which are not naturally present.

23. _____ You can store foods in the freezer for 6 months to a year.

24. _____ Potatoes should be refrigerated.

**Match the appliance to the phrase that best describes its use** (each answer, 2 points).

25. _____ can make the Belgian variety        a. crock pot

26. _____ has a mixing, rising and baking compartment        b. blender

27. _____ used to puree food        c. waffle iron

28. _____ serves as an extra burner to the stove        d. toaster

29. _____ can function as an extra oven        e. toaster oven

30. _____ used for slow cooking        f. bread machine

31. _____ warms and browns breads        g. electric fry pan

**Match the ingredient to the phrase that describes its function** (each answer, 2 points).

32. _____ gives richness and sweetness        a. eggs

33. _____ primary ingredient        b. flour

34. _____ gives interest to recipe        c. fat

35. _____ makes dough rise        d. leavening agent

36. _____ adds nutrients as well as richness        e. sweetener

37. _____ adds richness and flavor, helps in browning        f. seasoning

**Match the mixing and recipe terms to their definitions** (each answer, 3 points).

38. _____ cut into small pieces        a. fold

39. _____ beat ingredients to add air and increase volume        b. whip

40. _____ cook meat in an uncovered, shallow pan in an oven        c. braise

41. _____ mix ingredients together while preventing loss of air        d. simmer

42. _____ cook in liquid to just below the boiling point        e. chop

43. _____ cut into small cubes        f. dice

44. _____ cook in a small amount of water in a covered container        g. knead

45. _____ press dough with the palms of the hands, turning the dough slightly as you push it        h. roast

## HOME ECONOMICS LIFEPAC 3 ALTERNATE TEST

**Name** _____

**Date** _____

**Score** _____

64 / 80

**Answer** *true* or *false* (each answer, 2 points).

1. _____ Cholesterol is a plant material that humans cannot digest.

2. _____ Amino acids are building blocks used to make proteins.

3. _____ Vitamin C helps keep the gums and teeth healthy.

4. _____ Vitamin D helps promote proper digestion.

5. _____ Vitamin B helps clot the blood.

6. _____ Iron is important in the prevention of anemia.

7. _____ Broccoli and green peppers are good sources of Vitamin C.

8. _____ Milk is the best source of protein.

9. _____ Children should start using the Dietary Guidelines for Americans and the Food Guide Pyramid at two years of age.

10. _____ Diabetes is the result of abnormal glucose levels.

11. _____ A person is said to be obese if their weight exceeds 20% of their ideal weight.

12. _____ The most important characteristic of prepared cereal is flavor.

13. _____ Vegetables and fruits are classified by how they are grown.

14. _____ If you double the vegetable recipe, increase the liquids, herbs and spices by less than 1/3.

15. _____ The character of cheese depends on its variety alone.

16. _____ Air is the leavening agent for an angel food cake.

17. _____ The function of fat in a pastry is to provide tenderness, richness and flakiness.

18. _____ Cooking in salted water causes vegetables to lose their vitamin content.

19. _____ Teens need at least three servings of milk each day.

20. _____ Tender cuts of beef are best when cooked by moist heat methods.

21. _____ Bouillon is a rich creamy soup.

22. _____ Yeast ferments carbon dioxide gas that leavens the flour proteins in bread.

23. _____ Grade refers to the eating quality of beef.

24. _____ Roasting is a dry heat method of cooking where you cook directly under or over the source of heat.

25. _____ A molded cookie is baked as a sheet in a shallow pan.

26. _____ Vegetables grown underground should be cooked in an uncovered pan.

27. _____ Food should be served counterclockwise.

28. _____ The compromise style of service is a combination of the Russian and one other style.

29. _____ The family style of service is where the food is passed around the table and everyone helps himself.

30. _____ Table service is defined as the manner in which the foods are served at the table.

**Short Answer** (each answer, 5 points).

31. List the food pyramid groups and give the recommended number of servings for the average adult.

_____

_____

_____

_____

_____

_____

_____

32. Describe the qualities of a good pastry.

_____

_____

_____

33 Cooking is an art that appeals to the five senses. Explain.

_____

_____

_____

34. Draw and label a proper place setting. It should include a dinner plate, bread plate with knife, dinner knife, spoon, soupspoon, dinner fork, salad fork, dessert fork and spoon, napkin, water glass and beverage glass.

## HOME ECONOMICS LIFEPAC 4 ALTERNATE TEST

**Name** _____

**Date** _____

**Score** _____

80 / 100

**Fill in the blank** (each answer, 3 points).

1. Clothes are sorted by color, fabric, _____ and amount of soil.

2. Zippers should be _____ on garments before washing.

3. A soak in _____ is good for removal of blood stains.

4. Knits, laces and sheers require a _____ washing cycle.

5. Which natural fiber needs mothproofing? _____

6. _____ is an inert carbohydrate found in the cell walls of wood, cotton, hemp, etc.

7. A _____ is a set of written or unwritten rules of what should or should not be worn by a group of people.

8. Camouflaged suits, raincoats and bullet-proof vests are examples of clothes worn for _____ .

9. _____ is one's position or rank in comparison to others.

10. Blue, blue-green and green are an example of a (n) _____ color scheme.

11. _____ is the design principle that applies to the spatial or size relationships of all the parts to one another and to the whole.

12. White, black and gray are examples of _____ colors.

**Answer** *true* **or** *false* (each answer, 2 points).

13. _____ A side seam is an example of a stress seam.

14. _____ The best hand-stitch for hemming heavy fabrics and knits is the catch-stitch.

15. _____ Beeswax is a non-woven bonding agent.

16. _____ Needles that are medium-length with round eyes and sharp points are known as "steels."

17. _____ Acetate is a generic name.

18. _____ Fiberglass is a synthetic.

19. _____ Polyester is used for permanent press fabrics.

20. _____ Almost all synthetics are uncomfortable in hot and humid weather.

21. _____ Silk is more apt to wrinkle than cotton.

22. _____ Orange is a secondary color.

23. _____ Blue is a secondary color.

24. _____ Adornment refers to decoration and beauty.

25. _____ Modesty in dress is an important part of being concerned for others.

26. _____ The style of a garment is shown by its design or shape.

27. _____ Paris fashions set the trends in men's clothing.

28. _____ Red and green is an example of a complimentary color scheme.

29. _____ Formal balance is asymmetrical.

30. _____ If you are short you should wear vertical lines.

31. _____ If you are tall you should wear tiny prints.

**Select by underlining the correct answer from the two choices given for each description** (each answer, 2 points).

32. (Empire or Princess)     A dress style that has a high waistline.

33. (Gored or Dirndl)     Gathered only slightly.

34. (Harem or Knickers)     Flared pants that are gathered at the ankle.

35. (Raglan or Cap)     Short sleeve just covering the shoulder.

36. (Jewel or Cowl)     Simple, round neckline.

37. (Rolled or Chelsea)     First stands up from the neck edge, then falls down to rest on the garment.

38. (Dickey or Cravat)     Detachable shirt front.

**Define the following words** (each answer, 6 points).

39. value

_____

_____

_____

40. wardrobe

_____

_____

_____

# HOME ECONOMICS LIFEPAC 5 ALTERNATE TEST

**Name** _____

**Date** _____

**Score** _____

78 / 98

**Answer** *true* **or** *false* (each answer, 4 points).

1. _____ The balance wheel is used for starting and stopping the sewing machine.
2. _____ Tension disc and thread guides control the flow of threads.
3. _____ The bed is the metal spool that holds the lower thread used in stitching.
4. _____ The bobbin thread is the thread that is pulled in gathering.
5. _____ The most common amount for a seam allowance is 3/8″.
6. _____ The crosswise grain line is the grain line with the most stretch.
7. _____ Essential to a well fitting garment are accurate measurements.
8. _____ The raw edge of the fabric is called the selvage.
9. _____ Extra fabric is needed for plaids, stripes, and one-way designs.
10. _____ The selvage runs parallel with the lengthwise grain.

**Matching: Not all of the words will be used. Select the best answer** (each answer, 4 points).

11. _____ two close parallel lines
12. _____ broken line
13. _____ distance between the cutting line and the seam line.
14. _____ decorative stitch done on the right side of the garment.
15. _____ machine stitch to secure beginning and end of row.
16. _____ a way to finish and strengthen curved edges of garment.
17. _____ the side of the fabric intended to be seen.
18. _____ crosswise threads of the fabric
19. _____ should be consulted during construction.
20. _____ used to hold 2 pieces of fabric together temporarily.

a. alteration symbol
b. backstitch
c. basting stitch
d. blind-stitch
e. facing
f. Mom
g. pattern guide sheet
h. seam allowance
i. seam line symbol
j. right
k. top stitching
l. warp
m. woof

**Short answer** (each answer, 3 points).

21. The fabric is grain perfect if it has these three characteristics.

   a._____
   b._____
   c._____

22. What three things do you need to know to figure how much fabric you need to purchase?

   a._____
   b._____
   c._____

# HOME ECONOMICS LIFEPAC 6 ALTERNATE TEST

**Name** _____

**Date** _____

**Score** _____

78 / 97

**Matching** (each answer, 2 points).

| | | | |
|---|---|---|---|
| 1. | _____ claw and ball | a. | Louis XV |
| 2. | _____ gold-stenciled and black painted | b. | German Peasant |
| 3. | _____ Scandinavian design | c. | Queen Anne |
| 4. | _____ cabriole leg | d. | Victorian |
| 5. | _____ eclectic | e. | Shaker |
| 6. | _____ Pennsylvania Dutch | f. | Alvar Alto |
| 7. | _____ cast-iron stove | g. | Hitchcock |

**Answer** *true* **or** *false* (each answer, 2 points).

8. _____ Duncan Phyfe was the most famous American furniture maker.

9. _____ Louis Tiffany led the Art Nouveau movement in the U.S.

10. _____ Wainscot is a type of wood paneling used first by the Americans.

11. _____ Hepplewhite is known for his design of the shield-back chair.

12. _____ Cool colors create a cheerful and inviting mood in a room.

13. _____ Softwood comes from trees that keep their leaves all year long.

14. _____ Shutters are the least expensive type of window treatment.

15. _____ Furniture with different kinds of wood can be used in the same room.

16. _____ Mini-prints create a sense of space in a room.

17. _____ Plants may be used as a window covering.

18. _____ Local lighting is the preferred lighting for the kitchen.

19. _____ Walls in a room can be a focal point or neutral background.

20. _____ The sun does not really have a significant influence on you choice of wallpaper.

21. _____ Artwork should be hung so that the bottom of the piece is just below eye level.

22. _____ The tallest object should be placed first for an asymmetrical table arrangement.

23. _____ The first thing to consider when deciding on a table arrangement is the angle from which it will be viewed.

**Matching** (each answer, 3 points).

24. _____ Which of the following are primary colors?

    a.  red, blue, yellow        b.  orange, green, purple      c.  red, yellow, purple

25. _____ Tight, curved lines indicate.

    a.  strength and dignity        b.  action, movement        c.  springiness

26. _____ Which of the following is a good resilient floor covering?

    a.  vinyl             b.  wood             c.  ceramic

27. _____ shows a pleasing relationship among all parts resulting in harmony to the design as a whole.

    a.  Scale            b.  Balance          c.  Proportion

28. _____ Which of the following is **not** an example of a curtain?

    a.  café              b.  pinch-pleat        c.  Priscilla

29. _____ What historical event influenced the furniture style during the reign of Louis XVI?

    a.  French Revolution       b.  Industrial Revolution      c.  Excavation of Pompeii

30. _____ Which of the following are examples of softwood?

    a.  maple, oak, redwood      b.  pine, cedar, redwood      c.  mahogany, cherry, maple

31. _____ Which of the following is **not** an example of a three-dimensional object?

    a.  picture          b. lamp            c.  artwork

32. _____ Which of the following is least used for making rugs?

    a.  wool             b.  olefin           c.  acrylic

33. _____ Small pieces of fabric applied as decorative trimming by hand or machine are?

    a.  trapunto         b.  quilting         c.  appliqué

34. _____ Which of the following is **not** a result of the Industrial Revolution?

    a.  Federal style of        b.  better quality of       c.  furniture made by machines
        furniture                  furniture

**Matching: Answers may be used more than once** (each answer, 2 points).

35. _____ light or neutral-colored objects        a.   makes a room look larger

36. _____ large patterns on wall and ceiling      b.   makes a room look smaller

37. _____ windows and doors                  c.   makes a room look shorter

38. _____ rhythm                           d.   progression of tints and shades of color

39. _____ emphasis                        e.   reflect light

40. _____ painted dark or bright colors        f.   focal point

41. _____ light values

42. _____ dark values

43. _____ light colors

# HOME ECONOMICS LIFEPAC 7 ALTERNATE TEST

**Name** _____

**Date** _____

**Score** _____

80 / 100

**Multiple choice** (each answer, 3 points).

1. You can accommodate more people at an open house than your house will hold by? _____
   a. hoping everyone won't come that said they would
   b. requesting some of your close friends take the lead and leave early
   c. staggering the invitation hours

2. Which of the following is true about a shower? _____
   a. usually given by a family member
   b. gifts are usually expensive and extravagant for a bridal shower
   c. a baby shower is usually given about a month before the baby is due

3. Bill dropped in to see Sarah. How long is it appropriate for him to stay? _____
   a. 10 minutes          b. 15 minutes          c. 30 minutes

4. Which of the following is **not** an appropriate gift for a couples shower? _____
   a. lingerie            b. towels              c. tools

5. Tim is at a formal dinner with Jane. Everyone is being seated at the table. Tim has assisted Jane in sitting down. He notices that May who is to sit next to him on his other side is still standing and her escort has already sat down. Which of the following is the best solution to Tim's dilemma? _____
   a. Sit down and hope that May's escort finally helps to seat her.
   b. Remain standing until May finally sits down.
   c. Offer to help May be seated.

6. Terri has discovered a fishbone in her mouth. What should do with it? _____
   a. Remove the fishbone with her thumb and forefinger.
   b. Spit the fishbone into her napkin.
   c. Place the fishbone on her fork and put it on the side of her plate.

7. What is the signal that the meal has begun? _____
   a. The hostess takes her first bite of food.
   b. The hostess unfolds her napkin.
   c. neither a or b

8.  John is flying to New York to give a speech at a business conference. His seat mate on the plane is talking nonstop to him. John needs to polish his presentation for his meeting. What can he do about his talkative seat mate? _____

    a.  Offer his seat mate a magazine or book.

    b.  Tell his seat mate to "Be Quiet!"

    c.  Ask the stewardess to move him to another seat.

9.  Brian wants to take Anna out for pizza but is short on funds. What would be the most appropriate plan of action? _____

    a.  Don't ask Anna out until he has saved up enough money to pay for the date.

    b.  Call Anna and honestly explain his money situation and ask her if she would want to go with him Dutch treat.

    c.  Call Anna and ask her to pay this time, promising that he will pay next time.

10. The best way to fix a clogged drain is to? _____

    a.  Clean mounting nut

    b.  Use the plunger

    c.  Clean aerator screen

11. What do you do if the toilet is overflowing? _____

    a.  Shut off the main source of water

    b.  Use the plunger

    c.  Check the flapper

**Answer** *true* **or** *false* (each answer, 3 points).

12. _____ A party is a good time to make the new recipe you have been wanting to try.

13. _____ A reception is usually in the afternoon.

14. _____ The two priorities for the guest quarters are privacy and cleanliness.

15. _____ The best way to see if your guest room is comfortable is to have the guests fill out a questionnaire before they leave.

16. _____ You should plan extensive activities for your guests so there is not a moment of boredom.

17. _____ You should expect to be with your guests all of the time.

18. _____ As a guest you should always insist upon helping the host.

19. _____ It is the job of the host to get the conversation rolling.

20. _____ You should cut all of your meat at one time.

21. _____ If you spill on the tablecloth, it is best to cover the spill with a plate or something.

22. _____ A woman traveling alone would be wise to carry a cellular phone.

23. _____ You should make a reservation when dining at a fancy restaurant.

24. _____ The three main issues that come up on a date are who initiates the date, you controls the date, and who pays.

25. _____ The first step in cleaning the house is to dust.

26. _____ You should buff furniture in a circular motion.

27. _____ Regular vacuuming is the best way to maintain your carpets.

28. _____ Vinegar and baking soda make a good solution for cleaning water stains on faucets.

29. _____ Improper tire inflation is the major cause of tire failures.

30. _____ The oil should be changed in your car every 3,000 miles.

**Short answer** (10 points).

31. How are hospitality and Christian character related?

_____

_____

_____

# HOME ECONOMICS LIFEPAC 8 ALTERNATE TEST

**Name** _____

**Date** _____

**Score** _____

80 / 100

**Answer** *true* **or** *false*. If the statement is true, write *true* on the blank provided. If the statement is false, replace the underlined words with the correct response and write it in the blank provided (each answer, 5 points).

1. _____ A resume that concentrates on past skills and responsibilities is a <u>functional</u> resume.

2. _____ Good posture can send a message of <u>confidence</u>.

3. _____ It is a good idea to be <u>on time</u> for a job interview.

4. _____ You should dress <u>conservatively</u> for a job interview.

5. _____ Employers rely <u>only</u> on the information given on an application form when deciding whether or not to hire an applicant.

6. _____ Forms that answer questions Who? What? When? Why? How Much? and How many? are called <u>descriptive forms</u>.

7. _____ List of insurance companies, policy numbers and amount should be stored in an <u>expandable folder</u>.

8. _____ Two retirement plans that companies offer are 401(k) and <u>IRA</u>.

9. _____ The tax form you fill out and give to your employer is the <u>W-2</u> form.

10. _____ The annual amount you pay for insurance is called the <u>premium</u>.

11. _____ Your home owner's insurance covers all your personal possessions for up to <u>60%</u> of the amount of insurance on the building.

12. _____ A <u>budget</u> is a plan for using income to meet your needs, wants, and goals.

13. _____ Banks make their money from <u>interest on loans</u>.

14. _____ Signed contracts are <u>legally binding</u>.

15. _____ You can be held <u>reliable</u> for any preexisting damage to the apartment if you sign the lease without noting these damages.

16. _____ A <u>joint-tenancy</u> plan guarantees the surviving owner automatically inherits your share of the property at the time of your death.

17. _____ Retirement plans, life insurance and gifts can be set up with a designated <u>beneficiary</u>.

18. _____ Checking information to see if it is accurate and complete is called <u>reconciling</u>.

19. _____ An agreement with a store that allows a customer to pay for purchases at a later date is a <u>charge account</u>.

20. _____ A home loan is an example of <u>long-term</u> credit.

# HOME ECONOMICS LIFEPAC 9 ALTERNATE TEST

**Name** _____

**Date** _____

**Score** _____

80 / 100

**Answer** *true* or *false* (each answer, 3 points).

1. _____ Babies discover their fingers, feet and toes at three or four months.

2. _____ Preschoolers are afraid to be separated from their parents.

3. _____ A two-year old might have an imaginary playmate.

4. _____ Young school age children have a 2000 word vocabulary.

5. _____ Classification skills and reasoning ability start developing at three years old.

6. _____ The two-year old understands the meaning of sharing.

7. _____ The four-year old often experiences hero worship.

8. _____ Each child should be expected to earn your love.

9. _____ Most children are potty trained by age 2 1/2.

10. _____ A young child should have 3-5 servings of milk each day.

11. _____ Submission needs to be learned in the toddler stage of his life.

12. _____ Discipline should be done in private, with love and gentleness.

13. _____ The three areas of discipline are instruction, nurture and admonition.

14. _____ Four-year old's need toys which encourage make-believe play.

15. _____ The three-year old needs toys he can experiment with and share with friends.

16. _____ Children ages four through eight are at the symbolic stage of art.

17. _____ The three most common highly contagious children's diseases are chicken pox, head lice and measles.

18. _____ Baking soda is good to use on an ant bite.

19. _____ Anaphylactic shock is most commonly in response to bee stings, medications or food.

20. _____ All children should be taught "stop, drop and roll."

**Short Answer** (each answer, 5 points).

21. How can you teach kindness to a three-year old during Sunday School?

_____

_____

22. How can you teach a two-year old to pray?

_____

_____

**Define and give the age group of each of the following types of play** (each answer, 5 points).

23.   a.   solitary play    _____

       b.   imaginative play    _____

       c.   parallel play    _____

       d.   cooperative play    _____

**Essay.** (10 points).

24.    Select an age level and give the characteristics for the child's physical, social, intellectual and spiritual development.

       _____

       _____

       _____

       _____

       _____

       _____

       _____

       _____

       _____

       _____

       _____

       _____

       _____

       _____

# HOME ECONOMICS LIFEPAC 10 ALTERNATE TEST

**Name** _____

**Date** _____

**Score** _____

80 / 100

**Define relationship** (9 points).

1. _____
   _____
   _____

**Define friend** (9 points).

2. _____
   _____
   _____

**Answer** *true* **or** *false* (3 points).

3. _____ Discussions for settling differences should begin and end with prayer.

4. _____ Your parents allowing you to use the car demonstrates their trust in you.

5. _____ You can avoid jealousy of siblings by emulating them.

6. _____ Building a strong relationship with grandparents, helps them as much as it helps you.

7. _____ It is safe to assume that your boss knows you are accomplishing assigned tasks.

8. _____ A teacher serves as a counselor, encourager, and evaluator.

9. _____ Intimate knowledge about your private affairs could turn into a weapon for an over-ambitious co-worker.

10. _____ Nehemiah wept, prayed, and fasted for the people of the church.

11. _____ Courtesy and kindness are keys to any relationship.

12. _____ God exposes flaws in our role models to remind us that nobody is perfect.

13. _____ Teenage sex can result in alienation from family and friends.

14. _____ Once virginity is lost, it cannot be forgiven.

15. _____ Fidelity in marriage is not an absolute.

16. _____ How you live as a single person will affect your marriage relationship.

**Fill in the Blanks** (each blank, 5 points).

17. Family ministries of the church should result in families and marriages that _____ and _____.

18. A believer should expect his church to provide the following qualities for him and his family: teaches proper _____, ministers to the family and _____ in the community.

19.    Communication, _____, and _____ play important roles in
your relationship with your parents.

**Essay** (10 points).

20.    Distinguish between the world view and Christian view of marriage.

_____

_____

_____

_____

_____

_____

_____

_____

_____

_____

_____

_____

## SECTION ONE

1.1 Virtue is the resolve to stay pure.

Knowledge is an intellectual aspect involving feeding the thought life to do right.

Temperance involves self-control towards yourself.

Patience is the self-control you show toward others.

1.2 The beginning point upon which the qualities of 2 Peter 1: 2-7 are built is salvation.

1.3 Biblical principles are those principles based on Scripture and are never changing. Personal preferences change from generation to generation, culture to culture and day to day. Personal preferences are not addressed by the Scriptures in a clear or definite manner.

1.4 a. b
   b. p
   c. b
   d. p
   e. b
   f. p

1.5 a. Individuality: we are created in God's image, yet we are complex and unique.

   b. Self-government: teaches us to control ourselves concerning behavior and discipline.

   c. Christian character: teaches us to do everything we do to the best of our abilities and to honor God.

   d. Conscience: our conscience is our safe guide to do right and must be trained and filled with Godly thoughts.

1.6 Any four: heredity, environment, religion, where you live, family size or status and role models.

1.7 Adult check

1.8 Answers will vary

1.9 Either order:
   a. temperament
   b. character

1.10 Answers will vary

1.11 Answers will vary

1.12 Answers will vary

1.13 Answers will vary

1.14 Answers will vary

**SECTION TWO**

2.1    Health is the general condition of the body or mind with reference to soundness and vigor.

2.2    Hygiene is a condition or practice conducive to the preservation of health, as cleanliness.

2.3    Health is state of wellness and hygiene is the method or technique for maintaining that state of wellness.

2.4    You need it to be active, it catches the eye and makes you attractive.

2.5    The Biblical principle that is important for maintaining good health is self-government.

2.6    Adult Check

2.7    Either order:
       a. nutrition
       b. physical fitness

2.8    The key to proper nutrition is a well-balanced diet.

2.9    The food pyramid replaced the "four food groups" for determining a well-balanced diet.

2.10   The foods represented by the widest color of the food pyramid are the foods from which we should eat the largest amount.

2.11   Any order:
       a. muscle strength
       b. muscle endurance
       c. flexibility
       d. aerobic endurance

2.12   c.  eating too little

2.13   e.  fat

2.14   a.  carbohydrates

2.15   d.  sugar

2.16   b.  salt

2.17   Adult check

2.18   Answers will vary

2.19   You should shower or bathe at least once a day.

2.20   Moisture given off by the body combined with dirt and soiled clothing, warmed by the skin.

2.21   A regular deodorant prevents odor; an antiperspirant stops wetness.

2.22   Any order:
       a. fresh breath
       b. removes food particles
       c. removes plaque
       d. prevents cavities

2.23   Answers will vary

2.24   The focal point of the face is the eyes.

2.25   Makeup should be used in moderation in order to enhance your own natural beauty and not hide it. For example, eye makeup should be used only to enhance the color, size, depth, spacing and sparkle of your eyes.

2.26   Lipstick is used not only to intensify color, but it can also be used effectively to perfect the shape and proportion of your mouth.

2.27   Adult check

2.28   Adult check

2.29   Adult check

2.30   Adult check

2.31   Adult check

2.32   Adult check

2.33   Adult check

2.34   Adult check

2.35   Adult check

2.36   Adult check

2.37   Adult check

**SECTION THREE**

3.1 <u>Godliness</u> is our effort to be more Christ-like.

<u>Brotherly kindness</u> infers right actions and attitudes toward other Christians.

<u>Charity</u> denotes right actions and attitudes toward all men.

3.2 True

3.3 True

3.4 False

3.5 False

3.6 The fruits of the Spirit are love, joy, peace, long-suffering, gentleness, goodness, faith, meekness and temperance.

3.7 Answers will vary

3.8 Answers will vary

3.9 An important lesson learned by reading James 1:19, 20 is if we listen before speaking, anger may be avoided, opening the gates of true communication.

3.10 Good eye contact while conversing with someone shows genuine interest and concern for what they are saying.

3.11 According to Matthew 12:36, we are accountable to God for our conversation.

3.12 The most important person in a conversation is the other person.

3.13 Answers will vary:
<u>Proverbs 31:26</u> states that we should speak with wisdom and kindness.

<u>Philippians 4:8</u> admonishes us to speak in truth, honesty, purity, lovely and a good report (no gossip).

<u>Colossians 4:6</u> tells us our speech needs to be gentle but truthful.

3.14 Conversational "sweeteners" are the use of polite words such as "thank-you," "please," and "pardon me."

3.15 Strive to be friendly and <u>smile</u> in your conversation.

3.16 "Mother, I would like to introduce you to my friend, Sally."

**SECTION ONE**

1.1     the sink, stove and refrigerator

1.2     2 feet

1.3     4-7

1.4     between the range and the refrigerator

1.5     U-shaped kitchen layout, because it has the best work-triangle space.

1.6     The equipment and cabinets are placed on two adjacent sides; when possible the sink and the range are placed at right angles to one another.

1.7     to preserve nutrients and to keep food cold

1.8     6 months to a year

1.9     Either order:
       a. gas
       b. electric

1.10    The convection oven circulates hot air around the oven cavity, is more energy-efficient and cuts cooking time 30% and use reduced temperatures.

1.11    A garbage disposal is a piece of equipment that cuts garbage into tiny pieces that can be washed through the drain into the sewer.

1.12    it eliminates odor causing, bug attracting garbage from trash cans

1.13    cabinets

1.14    durability, aesthetics, ease of cleaning, comfortable to walk or stand on

1.15    Immersible means that an object can be placed under water.

1.16    A toaster is an electric appliance that will warm or brown breads.

1.17    A blender is an electric appliance used to puree soups, sauces and other liquids.

1.18    A crock pot is an electric appliance used for slow cooking stews and sauces.

1.19    A waffle iron is an electric appliance used to make waffles.

1.20    A stand mixer has a more powerful motor, so it can be used for heavier mixing than a hand-held mixer and it allows freedom of your hands.

1.21    mixing, rising and baking

1.22    electric skillet

1.23    coffee

1.24    electric percolator and drip

1.25    measuring dry ingredients, Examples: flour, sugar, cereal. (Answers may vary for the examples of ingredients)

1.26    clear glass measuring cups

1.27    liquids and dry ingredients

1.28    internal

1.29    sturdiness, heat conductivity and efficient retention of heat

1.30    the juices will evaporate and burn

1.31    bake breads or meatloaf

1.32    muffins and cupcakes

1.33    metal and glass

1.34    A good pan should be heavy enough to sit securely on the burner, not too heavy to lift and heavy base for gentle, even heat distribution.

1.35    fry foods

1.36    keep in nutrients and flavor

1.37    double boiler

1.38    3″ paring knife, a 5″ or 6″ utility knife, an 8″ or 9″ steak and poultry knife, a 9″ roast slicer, an 8″ or 10″ French cook's or chef's knife, and a Waverly edge bread and cake knife. (*Note:* listing knife sizes is optional.)

1.39    Waverly edge; a tomato knife has a Waverly edge.

1.40    double Waverly edge and a curved tip

1.41    Metal and grind of the blade, and by the type of handle and how it is attached.

1.42    stainless steel

1.43    Tang is the part of the blade that extends into the handle.

1.44    Adult check

1.45    Cover the flames with a pot lid, apply baking soda or salt. Never use water.

1.46    Turn off the heat and keep the door closed.

1.47    the plug from the outlet

1.48    empty the crumb tray

1.49    Answers will vary. Some examples found in the reading are: Keep cords from hanging down, block electric sockets, lock up chemicals, keep knives and small appliances out of their reach.

**SECTION TWO**

2.1     Adult check

2.2     add flavor, texture, richness, thickening/leavening and stronger framework

2.3     white granulated, brown and powdered

2.4     corn syrup

2.5     Bread flours are specifically used for bread and can make other recipes too tough.

2.6     salt and leavening

2.7     They all have different characteristics that could affect the final outcome.

        (Answers may vary) Example: lard is softer and richer than butter and will make flakier, more tender biscuits, or, low fat butter contains too much water to be suitable for baking or making candies.

2.8     the combination of warmth, sugar and liquid produce carbon dioxide that causes the dough to rise

2.9     water and milk

2.10    interest

2.11    False

2.12    True

2.13    False

2.14    False

2.15    True

2.16    read at eye level while cup is on a flat surface

2.17    16 ounces

2.18    Adult check: see that the student circled each word in the Word Search.

        a.  blend

        b.  fold

        c.  stir

        d.  cream

        e.  process

        f.  whip

        g.  cut in

        h.  mix

2.19    Unscramble the Words

        1.  broil - d

        2.  flute - h

        3.  blanch - b

        4.  dissolve - f

        5.  preheat - g

        6.  melt - c

        7.  julienne - i

        8.  cool - e

        9.  brown - j

        10. braise - a

2.20    Crossword Puzzle:

        Across:

        1.  baste

        4.  mince

        9.  marinate

        10. toss

        11. dough

        13. glaze

        15. scald

        Down:

        1.  batter

        2.  strain

        3.  simmer

        5.  caramelize

        6.  roast

        7.  stew

        8.  knead

        12. grease

        14. steam

**SECTION THREE**

3.1 False

3.2 False

3.3 False

3.4 False

3.5 True

3.6 False

3.7 True

3.8 False

3.9 True

3.10 False

3.11 True

3.12 convenience store

3.13 thrift store/day old store

3.14 supermarket

3.15 specialty store

3.16 Farmer's market

3.17 warehouse

3.18 Answers will vary.

3.19 Beef and Vegetable Stew
a. the front of the label
b. the list of ingredients.

3.20 Vegetable and Beef Stew

3.21 Beef

3.22 Any two of the following: nutritional value, preparation directions, total weight, number of servings, serving suggestions, storing information.

3.23 a. Fortified is the quantity of one or more nutrients, naturally present in a lesser amount, which has been increased.

b. Enriched is the addition of one or more nutrients which are not naturally present.

3.24 Standard

3.25 it slows their growth

3.26 meat drawer

3.27 vegetable drawer

3.28 a. Cured is a method or process of preserving meat or fish, etc. as smoking or salting.

b. Deterioration is the process by which something (food) becomes worse; lower in character, quality, or value.

3.29 unwrapped meat

3.30 No

3.31 in the pod in the refrigerator

3.32 6 months

3.33 3-5 days

3.34 the water has been removed

3.35 -18° C to -9° C (-0.4° F to 15.8° F)

3.36 in the refrigerator

3.37 the following should be checked:
a. tomato
d. peaches
e. avocados
h. plums

## SECTION ONE

1.1 Any order:
  a. proteins
  b. carbohydrates
  c. fats
  d. vitamins
  e. minerals
  f. water

1.2 animal foods

1.3 carbohydrates

1.4 incomplete

1.5 proteins

1.6 fats

1.7 fiber

1.8 fats

1.9 activities

1.10 carbohydrates

1.11 False

1.12 False

1.13 True

1.14 True

1.15 True

1.16 growth

1.17 cannot be stored by the body

1.18 C

1.19 B

1.20 C

1.21 C

1.22 B

1.23 fat-soluble

1.24 A, green, yellow

1.25 D

1.26 bones, teeth

1.27 fortified milk

1.28 Vitamin E

1.29 helps to clot the blood

1.30 calcium and phosphorous

1.31 iron

1.32 iodine

1.33 fluorine

1.34 iron

1.35 sodium, chlorine, potassium

1.36 Any three: milk, milk products, yogurt, hard cheese, fish, green leafy vegetables

1.37 Either one: iodized salt, salt water fish

1.38 Minerals that are found only in small amounts in the body.

1.39 See Chart below: Answers may vary but should be as complete as possible.

| NUTRIENT | WHY NEEDED | SOURCES |
|---|---|---|
| Proteins | build and repair tissues, to promote growth, to furnish heat and energy and to assist in regulating body processes | meat, eggs, milk, fruits, vegetables and grains |
| Carbohydrates | energy | sugar, starch as in pasta, bread, rice, legumes, whole grains and vegetables |
| Fats | helps the body use vitamins A, D, E and K. Gives energy, helps in growth and development of healthy tissues | animal fat such as meat, butter, cream and milk and fish and vegetable oils |

| | | |
|---|---|---|
| Vitamin A | healthy skin and mucous membranes, sound teeth, strong bones and growth, especially night vision | dark green and yellow vegetables, such as spinach, winter squash, carrots, sweet potatoes, cantaloupe and apricots |
| B Vitamins | promotes growth, good appetite and proper digestion, keeps nervous system healthy and prevents irritability, helps keep healthy skin | whole grains and enriched breads and cereals, leafy green vegetables, legumes, meat, milk and eggs |
| Vitamin C | mends broken bones and heals wounds, fights infection, maintain healthy teeth and gums | fruits and vegetables, especially citrus fruits |
| Vitamin D | strong bones and teeth | fortified milk, cod liver oil and other fish, exposure to sunlight |
| Vitamin E | keeps oxygen in the body from destroying nutrients | vegetable oils, whole grain breads and cereals, eggs, organ meats and green leafy vegetables |
| Vitamin K | helps to clot the blood | green leafy vegetables, cauliflower, liver and eggs |
| Calcium and Phosphorous | formation of strong bones and teeth | milk and milk products, fish, green leafy vegetables |
| Iron | healthy red blood cells | liver, meat, fish, nuts, eggs, dried beans and peas and whole grain breads and cereals |
| Iodine | helps the thyroid gland produce a hormone that affects growth and weight (metabolism) | iodized salt, salt water fish |
| Fluorine | development of strong bones and teeth, prevention of tooth decay | added to toothpaste, small amounts found in meats, milk and eggs |
| Sodium, Chlorine, Potassium | helps keep right amount of fluid around and inside cells in your body; allows cells to take up nutrients from the blood | sodium and chlorine are found in salt; potassium in bananas, orange juice, green leafy vegetables and milk |
| Water | helps get rid of waste, control body temperature, majority of blood content, moves nutrients around the body | mountain streams, rain, snow, etc. |

1.40　Dietary Guidelines for Americans:

Any order:
   a. Eat a variety of foods.
   b. Balance the food you eat with physical activity-maintain or improve your weight.
   c. Choose a diet with plenty of grain products, vegetables and fruit.
   d. Choose a diet that includes oils but is low in fat, saturated fat, and cholesterol.
   e. Choose a diet moderate in sugars.
   f. Choose a diet moderate in salt and sodium.
   g. Avoid alcoholic beverages.

1.41　The food pyramid gives not only the nutrients needed for a healthy diet but specifies the amounts.

1.42　a wider color

1.43　See the chart below.

| FOOD GROUP | NUMBER OF SERVINGS | NUMBER OF SERVINGS FOR TEENS | NUTRIENT(S) |
|---|---|---|---|
| a. Breads, Cereals, Rice and Pasta | 4-10 (some LIFEPACs say 6–11) | 6 (some LIFEPACs say 9) | complex carbohydrates, B vitamins, minerals and fiber |
| b. Fruits | 2–4 | 3 | Vitamin C, fiber, other vitamins |
| c. Vegetables | 3–5 | 4 | fiber, Vitamins, especially A and C |
| d. Meat, Poultry, Fish, Dried Beans, Eggs and Nuts | 2–3 | 2–3 | protein, iron, zinc, B vitamins |
| e. Milk, Yogurt, Cheese | 2–3 | 3 | calcium, protein, Vitamin $B_{12}$ |
| f. Fats, Oils, Sweets | use sparingly | use sparingly | calories, but very few nutrients |

1.44　nutrients, energy

1.45　Any two: growth rate, breast-feeding, health, weight, stature, size, activity

1.46　2 years

1.47　2/3

1.48　density, 3

1.49　1/4 or 25%

1.50　Convenience foods are those prepared at home from foods already cooked or otherwise processed before reaching the retail stores.

1.51　calcium and Vitamin A and C, sodium

1.52　salt

1.53　glucose

1.54　protein

1.55　Obesity is when a persons body weight is more than 20% above his ideal weight.

1.56　young women

1.57　iron-deficiency anemia, thyroid gland

1.58　a deficiency in:
   a. Vitamin A, night vision loss
   b. Vitamin D, rickets
   c. Vitamin C, scurvy
   d. Vitamin $B_1$, beriberi
   e. Vitamin $B_{12}$, blood disorders

**SECTION TWO**

2.1   wheat, oats, corn, rice

2.2   prepared and cooked

2.3   crispness

2.4   cream of wheat and oatmeal

2.5   1/2 pound - because they will swell from 2 to 4 times during cooking.

2.6   to remove any loose starch with which it is coated.

2.7   if it is to be served hot, rinse with hot water, if it is to be served cold, rinse with cold water

2.8   Adult check: See question in student's book for instructions.

2.9   are grown

2.10   e.  leafy

2.11   b.  stem

2.12   d.  seed

2.13   a.  root

2.14   c.  flower

2.15   a.  root

2.16   d.  seed

2.17   c.  flower

2.18   e.  leafy

2.19   b.  stem

2.20   a.  root

2.21   d.  seed

2.22   e.  leafy

2.23   fresh

2.24   covered, uncovered

2.25   less than 1/2

2.26   because salt tends to draw the vitamins out of the vegetable and into the water

2.27   Adult check. (answers will vary)

2.28   trees

2.29   tall bushes

2.30   bushes

2.31   vines

2.32   plants close to the ground

2.33   extra heavy syrup

2.34   Adult check: Make sure fruit is fresh. Check to see that recipe is correctly written, following the seven steps given in LIFEPAC 2 recipe section.

2.35   Scalded milk is milk that has been heated until bubbles form a ring around the top.

2.36   add the tomato to the milk

2.37   Yogurt is a milk product low in fat, low in calories.

2.38   sour cream

2.39   protein and minerals

2.40   age

2.41   mold

2.42   high, low

2.43   False

2.44   Adult check: See specifications in the student's book. Check to see that recipe is correctly written, following the seven steps given in LIFEPAC 2 recipe section.

2.45   Beef crossword puzzle:
ACROSS:
  1.  three to twenty one days
  5.  panfrying
  6.  marbling
  9.  grade
  10.  roasting
  11.  broiling
  12.  panbroil
DOWN:
  1.  trim
  2.  dark reddish purple
  3.  aging
  4.  prime
  7.  gristle
  8.  braising

2.46   Any two: the grade, the appearance, the aging.

2.47   marbling, trim, gristle, color

2.48   the tenderness

2.49   dry heat, moist heat

2.50   the bone conducts heat

2.51   because fat that is too hot creates an unpleasant flavor

2.52   prick with a sharp-tined fork, if the juice rises clear, untinged with pink, it is cooked enough

2.53   it becomes flaky or when its translucency is gone

2.54 A marinade is a liquid in which meats, fish or vegetables are soaked before cooking.

2.55 it adds flavor

2.56 Adult check: See specifications in the student's book. Check to see that recipe is correctly written, following the seven steps given in LIFEPAC 2 recipe section.

2.57 stock based and mild based

2.58 Any order:

    a. Bouillon - clear soup or broth made from beef or chicken

    b. Bisque - rich cream soup made from pureed seafood, fish or vegetable.

    c. Chowder - mild based soup or stew using fish, seafood, or vegetables.

    d. Consommé - clear soup made from boiling meat bones and vegetables.

2.59 accompaniment

2.60 dessert or party salad

2.61 enhances flavor, color and taste, or binds the ingredients together

2.62 French-type, mayonnaise type and cooked-egg.

2.63 A garnish a food used to decorate food, making it more attractive. Any two: carrot curls, radish roses, parsley, tomato peel roses, lemon wedges, pickle fans, celery curls. Answers may vary.

2.64 Adult check: See specifications in the student's book. Check to see that recipe is correctly written, following the seven steps given in LIFEPAC 2 recipe section.

2.65 Any order:

    a. the texture of the baked cookie

    b. the consistency of the batter or dough

    c. the method used in shaping them

2.66   a. drop cookies: have a soft, drop batter consistency

    b. refrigerator cookies: are rich in shortening, shaped into blocks or rolls and put in refrigerator for several hours, then sliced and baked

    c. bar cookies: are baked as a sheet in a shallow pan, cut into squares

    d. molded cookies: are formed into small balls and flattened with a fork

    e. rolled cookies: require stiff dough, are rolled out and cut into fancy shapes

    f. pressed cookies: are a soft dough, squeezed from a cookie press to form fancy shapes

2.67 Adult check: See specifications in the student's book. Check to see that recipe is correctly written, following the seven steps given in LIFEPAC 2 recipe section.

2.68 Angel food cakes are made without shortening, while butter cakes are made with shortening.

2.69 Butter cakes shrink from the sides of the pan and all cakes spring back into place when lightly touched with the fingers.

2.70 air

2.71 Frosting are thicker than icings and used on cakes only. Icings are thinner and used on cakes, breads, coffee cakes and sweet rolls.

2.72 Adult check: See specifications in the student's book. Check to see that recipe is correctly written, following the seven steps given in LIFEPAC 2 recipe section.

2.73 Golden brown crust, uniform attractive edge, blistery pebbly surface, flaky when cut, should hold together when cut.

2.74 fats, carbohydrates

2.75   1. b. flour

    2. d. water

    3. c. salt

    4. a. fat

2.76 Adult check: See specifications in the student's book. Check to see that recipe is correctly written, following the seven steps given in LIFEPAC 2 recipe section.

2.77 c. liquid

2.78 f. sugar

2.79 a. flour

2.80 d. salt

2.81 b. yeast

2.82 elasticity and extensibility

2.83 mushroom, center

2.84 Adult check: See specifications in the student's book. Check to see that recipe is correctly written, following the seven steps given in LIFEPAC 2 recipe section.

**SECTION THREE**

3.1 Adult check for completion.

3.2 a. main dish
b. color, texture and flavor
c. season
d. needs and appetites

3.3 Any order:
a. appetizer
b. main course
c. dessert

3.4 Answers will vary but should address each of the five senses. The meal should taste good and incorporate at least 2 or 3 of the following tastes: sweet, sour, salty, bitter. The aroma (smell) of food cooking should be good. Bacon frying or popcorn popping appeals to the sense of hearing. Appropriate texture of foods, like smooth creamy pudding satisfies the sense of feeling. Food should also be appealing to look at, sight.

3.5 Adult check: Answers will vary. Students should use the chart provided in their books.

3.6 Adult check for completion and accuracy.

3.7 Adult check for completion.

## SECTION FOUR

4.1 Table service is the manner or way in which food is served at a table.

4.2 formal, informal

4.3 informal

4.4 Any order:
   a. blueplate
   b. family
   c. buffet

4.5 English, Russian

4.6 simple or elaborate menu, dining space, available table appointments, time available for serving and eating, number of guests, the occasion

4.7 blueplate

4.8 buffet

4.9 decreasing order of importance: main dish, vegetables, salad, breads, beverage

4.10 family

4.11 Russian

4.12 hostess

4.13 a. a <u>cover</u> is each person's place setting, including all the appointments he or she will need for the meal
   b. <u>compromise style</u> of service is a combination of English and one other service, usually the blueplate

4.14 Any order:
   a. appetizer
   b. soup
   c. fish
   d. meat or main dish
   e. salad
   f. dessert
   g. demitasse

4.15 yes

4.16 No more than 3

4.17 cutting edge of the knife is facing toward the plate

4.18 above the dinner plate

4.19 above the forks

4.20 water glass above knife, beverage glass to its right, then cup and saucer

4.21 adds beauty and color to your table setting

4.22 Adult check: Student demonstrates ability to set a proper place setting. You can use the diagram given in the student's book.

4.23 A place card is an individual card placed at each cover with the guest's name on it, indicating where he/she is to sit.

4.24 the right

4.25 person seated to the right of the host

4.26 counterclockwise

4.27 left, right

4.28 1/2 to 1 inch from the rim

4.29 before you serve the dessert

4.30 Adult check. The student should demonstrate his/her ability to wait a table for the two styles indicated.

4.31 Adult check: You may have to have the parent grade this activity. Charts and scales are given. Answers will vary.

## SECTION ONE

1.1 Answers will vary. Examples may be as follows: coats, sweaters, hats, gloves, sunglasses, raincoats, etc.

1.2 occupational hazards

1.3 modestly

1.4 face or countenance

1.5 <u>Status</u> is one's position or rank in comparison to others.

1.6 higher rank in society, along with social acceptance and peer approval

1.7 <u>Identification</u> is the process of establishing or describing who or what someone is or someone does.

1.8 Answers will vary. Examples may be as follows: uniform like a doctor or nurse, professional attire like a lawyer or businessman, service badge, construction worker, uniform of athletic team, gang member clothes, etc.

1.9 kethon, addereth

1.10 sackcloth

1.11 vivid colors such as white, purple, scarlet, blue, yellow or black

1.12 cultures

1.13 character, individuality

1.14 A <u>dress-code</u> is written or unwritten rules of what should or should not be worn by a group of people.

1.15 <u>Personality</u> is the total characteristics that distinguish an individual, especially his or her behavioral and emotional tendencies.

1.16 <u>Fashion</u> is whatever is favored at a given time by those who are regarded as up-to-date.

1.17 Must be in order.
a. New fashions are introduced and worn by fashion leaders.
b. Adaptations are worn by different people (styles are created in materials that everyone can afford).
c. Well established styles lead to mass acceptance.
d. Social saturation - everyone has it.
e. Over-used and becomes dull and boring.
f. Declines in popularity.

g. Eventually becomes obsolete - no one would be seen wearing it.
h. In about 20 years - the fashion will be revived.
i. Some changes from before, but the style is there and the fashion leaders wear them.

1.18 Hand made clothes meant fashions could last a decade; mass production of dresses in the same design has greatly reduced the time it takes to design and make the clothes to reach a large number of people.

1.19 it made the velvet suit popular

1.20 Any order:
a. women worked in factories
b. they needed simple and easy to maintain dresses or slacks

1.21 a. back fullness - fitted bodice with a full skirt and a puff in the back;
b. bell-shaped - fitted bodice with full skirt;
c. tubular - straight

1.22 Paris, London

1.23 Adult check

1.24 Adult check

1.25 A custom-designed garment is specifically made for a particular person, having a special fit, design, and fabric for the person who ordered it. A custom-made garment is not designed for a particular person although it is made for that person.

1.26 <u>High</u>-priced market includes an extremely small number of people who buy fashion clothing of unusual styles and colors. <u>Moderate</u>-priced market includes garments that are factory produced in small numbers with dependable brand names and good fabrics. <u>Lower</u>-priced market includes clothes mass produced in common styles, fabrics and colors.

1.27 It was thought that the hemline affected stock market indexes. Short hemline resulted in a rise in stocks and the long hemline resulted in a fall in stocks.

1.28    j.   darts

1.29    t.   retail

1.30    b.   black fullness silhouette

1.31    g.   couturier

1.32    z.   wholesale

1.33    v.   style

1.34    d.   bodice

1.35    p.   irregulars

1.36    y.   wardrobe

1.37    a.   avant-garde clothes

1.38    s.   price markets

1.39    f.   composite garments

1.40    l.   fashion leaders

1.41    c.   bell silhouette

1.42    o.   high fashion

1.43    k.   draped garments

1.44    x.   tubular silhouette

1.45    i.   custom-made

1.46    r.   overruns

1.47    w.   tailored garments

1.48    n.   fitted

1.49    e.   classic

1.50    q.   knock-offs

1.51    u.   seconds

1.52    m.   fashion piracy

1.53    h.   custom-designed

1.54    Adult check

## SECTION TWO

2.1 <u>hue</u>: the quality or characteristic by which we distinguish one color from another

2.2 primary hues, red, yellow, blue

2.3 primary hues, orange, green, purple or violet.

2.4 by mixing one primary and one adjacent secondary color together

2.5 any of the following: yellow-orange, red-orange, red-violet, blue-violet, blue-green, yellow-green

2.6 value

2.7 A tint is made by white being added to a hue and is higher in value than a shade in which black is added to a hue.

2.8 neutral

2.9 The intensity is the brightness or dullness of a color. Tones are hues with their complimentary color or gray added. Which reduces their intensity.

2.10 In any order: <u>monochromatic</u>, the use of various values and intensities of one color; <u>analogous</u>, the use of hues that are closely related to one another on the color wheel; <u>complementary</u>, the use of hues that are directly opposite one another on the color wheel.

2.11 line

2.12 texture

2.13 body lines, silhouette lines and detail lines

2.14 proportion

2.15 emphasis

2.16 rhythm

2.17 gradual increase or decrease in size, color, texture and numbers

2.18 False

2.19 False

2.20 True

2.21 False

2.22 Crossword Puzzle:

Across

1. cardigan
2. parka
5. lowered
9. cape
10. hood
13. dropped shoulder
16. harem
17. pullover
19. cap
21. tab
24. jabot
26. hood
27. middy
29. pleats
30. sleeveless
33. raglan
35. tent
36. scoop
39. windbreaker
40. fitted
41. convertible
42. bolero
43. sheath
44. yoke
45. halter

Down

1. culottes
2. palazzo
3. ascot
4. jeans
6. waistband
7. dirndl
8. gored
11. jewel
12. princess
14. poncho
15. empire
18. vest
20. pocket
22. blouson
23. jumpsuit
25. bateau
27. mandarin
28. blazer
30. straight
31. keyhole

**SECTION TWO con't.**

Down

32. knickers
34. tunic
37. chelsea
38. kimono
41. cowl

2.23   height
2.24   very large, very heavy
2.25   vertical, princess
2.26   pleats, gathers

2.27   horizontal
2.28   curved, diagonal/vertical
2.29   wear gently lowered necklines with ties or collars
2.30   weight
2.31   Dark, light
2.32   Bright
2.33   False
2.34   Adult check
2.35   Adult check

**SECTION THREE**

3.1   These must be in order:
    a. fiber production: raw materials are processed into various fibers
    b. yarn production: mills spin fibers into yarns
    c. fabric manufacturing: plants weave or knit yarns into fabrics
    d. fabric finishing: finishing is done by bleaching, dying, printing or applying special coatings

3.2   Natural, man-made

3.3   a. puff protecting seed of the cotton plant
    b. fibrous stock of the flax plant
    c. fine filament from which the silk worm spins his cocoon
    d. fleece of sheep

3.4   wool
3.5   linen
3.6   cotton, linen
3.7   Silk, wool

3.8   Wool
3.9   Linen
3.10   Cotton
3.11   Silk
3.12   Wool
3.13   Cotton
3.14   middle of the 19th century
3.15   20th century
3.16   Man-made natural fibers are made from cellulose or protein taken from natural sources. Synthetic fibers are made from chemicals.
3.17   Answers may vary. Examples: rayon, acetates
3.18   Answers may vary. Examples: nylon, acrylics, polyester, spandex
3.19   acrylic
3.20   Lycra
3.21   they would be uncomfortable in hot or humid weather
3.22   True

## SECTION FOUR

4.1    sharps

4.2    because they could damage or snag the fabric

4.3    emergency repair, permanent repair

4.4    one dark color from your basic wardrobe (brown, black, navy), white red, medium gray and a transparent monofilament

4.5    A monofilament is a clear single large filament of synthetic fibers.

4.6    removing cut threads

4.7    6″ scissors with one sharp-point, with sharp blades

4.8    60″

4.9    shank, flat or sew through

4.10   allows the button to sit on top of the buttonhole instead of crowding the inside and distorting the buttonhole

4.11   heavy, bulky

4.12   Adult check

4.13   hook and eye

4.14   snap

4.15   straight eye

4.16   the flat hooks will not slide out of the eye

4.17   Adult check

4.18   machine straight stitch

4.19   backstitch

4.20   stretch stitch

4.21   Any of the following: crotch, underarm, pockets

4.22   smaller stitches, two rows of stitching, machine reinforcements stitching

4.23   Adult check

4.24   emergency

4.25   permanent, dry-cleaned

4.26   slip-stitch

4.27   catch-stitch

4.28   blind-stitch

4.29   straight-stitched

4.30   Adult check

4.31   Care Labeling Rule, revised in 1984

4.32   does not use heat

4.33   remove accessories, clean out pockets, mend

4.34   turn shirts inside out - button top button

4.35   color, degree of soil

4.36   True

4.37   False

4.38   Answers within each section maybe in any order.

Cotton-hot water:
  a. 2 Cotton bath towels
  b. 2 Hand towels
  c. 2 Wash clothes
  d. Cotton dish clothes
  e. Cotton dish towels

Cotton/linen-warm/cool water
  a. Denim skirt
  b. Denim shirt
  c. Cotton corduroy pants
  d. Linen suits (preshrunk)

Delicates/knits
  a. Knit yellow/white basketball jersey
  b. Nylon pastel undergarments
  c. Light blue Spandex shorts
  d. Light blue knit jersey pullover
  e. Beige knit skirt
  f. Lavender negligee
  g. Nylon pastel blouse
  h. Light green swimsuit

Hand wash or gentle machine
  a. Wool blend dress
  b. Fiberglass curtains
  c. Arnel cheerleader skirt (pleats)

Permanent press-light colors
  a. Pink Dacron dress

  b. Tan dress pants (slacks)

  c. Pastel dress shirt

  d. Pastel floral dress

  e. Yellow Qiana blouse

  f. Lavender dress

Permanent press-dark colors
  a. Maroon slacks

  b. Navy blue shorts

  c. Red dress

  d. Black suit jacket (lightweight)

  e. Purple shirt

  f. Dark blue slacks

Large permanent press
  a. Fitted full bed sheet

  b. Flat full bed sheet

  c. 2 Large pillowcases

Large permanent press
(too large, needs its own load)
  a. Blanket

Dry clean
  a. Rayon dress

  b. Fleece coat

  c. Taffeta formal

  d. Polyester shell with silver sequins

4.39   ironing, pressing

4.40   tends to stretch fabric

4.41   used for things that must be slipped over for ironing

4.42   Test the temperature on some inner part of the garment with a pressing cloth placed over the garment

4.43   iron pillowcases from closed end toward hem.

4.44   the collar, sleeves, yokes, pockets and trimming

## SECTION ONE

1.1    shorter, finer

1.2    purpose, structure, thread

1.3    f.  double longs

1.4    d.  chenilles

1.5    c.  calyx-eyes

1.6    b.  betweens

1.7    g.  glovers

1.8    a.  ball-points

1.9    h.  sharps

1.10    e.  curved needles

1.11    2-3

1.12    thicker

1.13    True

1.14    flathead

1.15    bent-handle dressmaker

1.16    True

1.17    True

1.18    bottom

### Word Search Activity:

(words in parenthesis are not in the word search)

1.19    Bed

1.20    Head

1.21    Needle

1.22    Presser foot

1.23    Spool pin

1.24    Needle bar

1.25    Throat plate

1.26    Feed dogs

1.27    Stitch (regulator)

1.28    Bobbin

1.29    Shuttle

1.30    Slide plate

1.31    Hand wheel

1.32    Take-up lever

1.33    Reverse button

1.34    Pressure (regulator)

1.35    Tension (regulator)

1.36    Tension discs

1.37    Light

1.38    Adult check

1.39    Adult check

1.40    The following in any order

    a. never stand on a chair when having the hem of a garment measured

    b. keep the drawers or doors of the sewing machine storage cabinets closed to avoid bumping into them

    c. keep fingers away from the path of the sewing machine needle

    d. put pins and needles in a pin cushion, never in your mouth, on your clothes or in upholstered furniture

    e. keep sharp objects out of your lap

    f. arrange the electric cord of the machine on the floor so that it will not cause anyone to stumble

    g. when pressing, keep your hands away from the steam

    h. disconnect the cord from the wall or floor outlet before disconnecting it from the machine

    i. turn off the iron when not in use

**SECTION TWO**

2.1   even backstitch

2.2   basting

2.3   Any of the following seams that need more control: curved seams, seams with ease, set-in sleeves.

2.4   Either of the following seams that need less control: straight seams; such as side or shoulder seams.

2.5   In order:
   a. measure and mark for desired length
   b. fold raw edge back about 1/4″ - 1/2″ or finish raw edge using other methods. Press.
   c. fold back again to marked desired finished length.
   d. pin in place.
   e. stitch by hand or machine - stitches should be neat, 3/8″ - 1/2″ apart and invisible on outside.

2.6   running stitch

2.7   In order:
   a. 2 or 3 lengthwise stitches in same place
   b. blanket stitch over lengthwise stitches

2.8   tailor's tack

2.9   Adult check

2.10   Adult check

2.11   Adult check

2.12   Adult check

2.13   backstitch, tie thread ends

2.14   tie thread

2.15   to hold fabric layers together during fitting or permanent machine stitching

2.16   The longest possible, 6 stitches per inch

2.17   4-6, 1 single

2.18   narrow, finishes

2.19   to keep facing and seam allowances lying flat

2.20   trimming all the seam allowances to different widths in order to eliminate bulk

2.21   False

2.22   True

2.23   False

2.24   Adult check

2.25   Adult check

2.26   Adult check

2.27   Adult check

2.28   False

2.29   5/8″

2.30   notched, clipped

2.31   Any order:
   a. type and weight of fabric
   b. amount of wear and care
   c. whether or not seams will be seen

2.32   pinked

2.33   zigzag

2.34   self-enclosed, French, flat-felled

2.35   Adult check

2.36   Adult check

2.37   Adult check

2.38   Adult check

2.39   A <u>dart</u> is a short, tapered, stitched area that enables the garment to fit the figure.

2.40   wide, point

2.41   By back stitching at the wide end and tying the threads at the point.

2.42   A <u>tuck</u> is a stitched fold of fabric for decorative or shaping purposes.

2.43   Blind tucks meet, while spaced tucks have space between them.

2.44   <u>Pleats</u> are folds in fabric that provide controlled fullness.

2.45   <u>Gathering</u> is the process of pulling an amount of fabric into a smaller area, along a stitch in order to create soft even folds.

2.46   bobbin thread

2.47   to finish raw edges at garment openings

2.48   Adult check

2.49   Adult check

2.50   Adult check

2.51   Adult check

2.52   remove presser foot and attach zipper foot

2.53   left side seam of pants, skirts and dresses

2.54   Any of the following: jacket, vest or skirt

2.55   top-stitching

2.56   left over right

2.57   Adult check

2.58   (Optional) Adult check

2.59   Adult check

## SECTION THREE

| | |
|---|---|
| 3.1 | True |
| 3.2 | False |
| 3.3 | True |
| 3.4 | True |
| 3.5 | False |
| 3.6 | False |
| 3.7 | the natural waistline |
| 3.8 | around the fullest part, usually 7 - 9 inches below the natural waistline |
| 3.9 | around the fullest part of the upper arm |
| 3.10 | Stand straight against a wall. Hold a ruler on top of the head parallel to the floor. Walk away to measure your height. |
| 3.11 | the most prominent bone at the base of the neck to the natural waistline |
| 3.12 | along seam on inside of leg to the hem (or desired length) |
| 3.13 | full bust measurement |
| 3.14 | neck band size |
| 3.15 | Adult Check |
| 3.16 | Any four of the following in any order: pattern number, garment images, size, pattern company, the price. |
| 3.17 | Adult check |
| 3.18 | a.–e.  Adult check<br>f.  2 3/4 yards |
| 3.19 | four |
| 3.20 | Any five of the following: rayon blends, cotton blends, lightweight linen, challis, gingham, seersucker, gauze, allover eyelet. |
| 3.21 | 1 1/2 yards |
| 3.22 | size 14 |
| 3.23 | 3 3/8 yards |
| 3.24 | 2 1/4 yards |
| 3.25 | 1/2 yard |
| 3.26 | 1 - 4, 5 and 6, 9 and 10 |
| 3.27 | 1 - 5, 7, 8, 9, 10 |
| 3.28 | 3 and 4 |
| 3.29 | 5, 7, 8 |
| 3.30 | b.  fabric |
| 3.31 | c.  printed side of pattern up |
| 3.32 | a.  printed side of pattern down |

| | |
|---|---|
| 3.33 | False |
| 3.34 | True |
| 3.35 | True |
| 3.36 | False |
| 3.37 | As follows:<br>a. cutting line<br>b. seam line<br>c. grain line<br>d. buttonhole<br>e. dot<br>f. notch<br>g. fold line<br>h. dart<br>i. notches<br>j. alteration lines<br>k. stitch directional arrows |
| 3.38 | the fewest |
| 3.39 | jiffy |
| 3.40 | size |
| 3.41 | c.  presser foot |
| 3.42 | a.  fabric |
| 3.43 | c.  sheer and shiny |
| 3.44 | b.  medium-priced |
| 3.45 | Shrinking the material before it is used to make a garment. |
| 3.46 | Selvage is the woven edge of the fabric that runs parallel to the lengthwise grain. |
| 3.47 | Grain perfect is when the crosswise threads are a 90° angle to the lengthwise threads. |
| 3.48 | yes |
| 3.49 | warp |
| 3.50 | woof |
| 3.51 | Any order: straighten the material by bringing the woof perpendicular to the selvage |
| 3.52 | raw edges meet, selvages meet, fold is flat |
| 3.53 | Any order: thread, zippers, buttons, interfacing, trim |

## SECTION FOUR

4.1 Any order:
  a. fabric is folded off-grain - straighten grain
  b. dress pattern piece B with grainline is placed on fold - line move and place on grain
  c. dress pattern piece A with a fold line is placed on the selvages - place on fold line
  d. dress pattern piece A is not on the fabric for both layers since the material is folded off grain - straighten grain and place on fold
  e. neck facing D with fold line is placed on selvage - move to fold line
  f. arm facing E is partially off the raw edge of the fabric - place back on fabric
  g. arm facing E is off grain - place on grain
  h. neck facing C with a grain line is placed off-grain - place on grain
  i. neck facing C is overlapping dress B - move from overlapping

4.2 False

4.3 True

4.4 True

4.5 False

4.6 tailor's, tailor's

4.7 felt-tip pens

4.8 wrong

4.9 sheer, bulky

4.10 Adult check

4.11 In order:
  a. open
  b. toward the center
  c. to prevent fabric from stretching

## SECTION FIVE

5.1 - 5.3 Adult check

5.4 Construction checklist: Student Check Evaluation Form: Student Check and Adult check

**SECTION ONE**

1.1 Furniture from the reign of Louis XIV was grand and massive for large palaces and estates. Furniture from the reign of Louis XV was small and intimate. The change was due to the fact that most aristocrats had moved into small apartments.

1.2 The excavation of the ancient Roman city of Pompeii

1.3 Provincial furniture is cruder in proportion and not as finely made as the Paris pieces it copied. Provincial furniture was more practical in purpose.

1.4 German peasants; geometric shape, angular and heavy in cut, decorations painted on the furniture was flat although realistic objects like birds and flowers were used.

1.5 Any order:

　a. Moors

　b. Renaissance

　c. practicality

1.6 solid masculine appearance, dark, heavy, massive wood construction

1.7 c. Louis XVI

1.8 e. Provincial

1.9 b. Louis XV

1.10 h. Spanish

1.11 a. Louis XIV

1.12 f. German peasant

1.13 d. Napoleon

1.14 g. Biedermeier

1.15 Half-timbered is where the spaces between the heavy wood supports of the building (houses) are filled with stucco.

1.16 cabriole chair leg; made with the claw and ball at the bottom of the cabriole leg

1.17 simple chair with curved back and arms for comfort

1.18 Chinese

1.19 Any order:

　a. Adam Brothers

　b. Hepplewhite

　c. Sheraton

1.20 simple, graceful lines and distinct chair backs

1.21 shield-back chair

1.22 furniture was made by machine, cheapening the quality; introduction of new materials for attached ornamentation rather than carved

1.23 The use of what seems best from various sources.

1.24 pine wood, simpler, less decorative, practical, and space-saving

1.25 Any two of the following: drop-leaf table, table/chair, storage chest benches

1.26 Any two of the following: pewter bowls and mugs, copper and iron cooking utensils

1.27 Adams brothers, Hepplewhite, Sheraton

1.28 Duncan Phyfe

1.29 table legs, chair backs and sofa arms had gentle curves, legs of chairs and tables ended in animal feet, used decorations of lyre, cornucopia, garlands, scrolls, and rosettes

1.30 painted black with gold stenciled in patriotic symbols or country motif

1.31 Shaker was a religious sect of the 19th century who fled to America from England because of religious persecution. They lived in communes in New York, Connecticut, and Massachusetts.

1.32 simple, practical, functional, no embellishments, no stain or lacquer

1.33 Any two of the following: built-in cupboard and dressers, rockers, cast-iron stove

1.34 American style was more forbidding, and dark colored.

1.35 New Art

1.36 Louis Tiffany

1.37 lamps, vases, stained glass windows

1.38 tubular steel

1.39 office and lawn furniture

1.40 Ludwig Mies von der Rohe

1.41 Paris

1.42 Chrysler Building and Radio City Music Hall

1.43 Alvar Aalto

1.44 Italy

1.45 Saarinen

1.46 Adult check

## SECTION TWO

2.1 Adult check: use color wheel in the text

2.2 a. hue: the name of the color

b. intensity: brightness or dullness of a color

c. shade: hue plus black

d. tint: hue plus white

e. tone: hue plus gray

f. value: darkness or lightness of color

g. white: pure light

2.3 warm

2.4 Any one: red-purple, purple, blue-purple, blue, blue-green or green

2.5 warm colors are cheerful and inviting; cooler colors are more restful

2.6 bright colors stand out more, contrast of dark on light background make dark stand out more, can affect the appearance of the room proportions

2.7 2:3 proportion

2.8 floor

2.9 Any order:
a. room's purpose
b. location
c. personal taste

2.10 f. neutral

2.11 e. complementary

2.12 a. analogous

2.13 c. monochromatic

2.14 b. triad

2.15 d. extended analogous

2.16 to describe the outline of a form or shape.

2.17 Answers may vary, any two: sofa, bed, dining table, desk

2.18 Answers may vary, any two: book shelves, chest of drawers

2.19 e. horizontal lines

2.20 c. diagonal lines

2.21 f. tight, curved lines

2.22 g. vertical lines

2.23 b. delicate, fine lines

2.24 e. horizontal lines

2.25 g. vertical lines

2.26 a. curved lines

2.27 d. heavy lines

2.28 a three dimensional setting for furniture or furnishings

2.29 the surface covering of fabric, furniture and furnishings

2.30 False

2.31 a pleasing relationship among parts resulting in harmony to the design as a whole

2.32 The size of the parts of a design or a group of objects in comparison to each other.

2.33 scale

2.34 formal

2.35 Either of the following: use a larger, light-colored object to balance a smaller darker object; several small objects to balance one larger object.

2.36 Any order:
a. repeat a color, design, line or shape
b. varying the size of the shapes or lines in a sequence
c. using a progression of tints or shades of a color

2.37 The point of interest in a room.

2.38 Adult check

2.39 Adult check

2.40 Adult check

2.41 Adult check

2.42 Adult check

2.43 Adult check

**SECTION THREE**

3.1 no

3.2 Hardwood comes from trees that lose their leaves in the winter and softwood comes from trees that retain their leaves all year.

3.3 Any two of the following: maple, oak, cherry, walnut, mahogany

3.4 Any two of the following: pine, cedar, redwood

3.5 hardwood

3.6 A rug is a small or large floor covering that is often woven with a variety of decorative patterns of more than one color of fabric. A carpet is a room size fabric floor covering.

3.7 synthetic or acrylic

3.8 Any two: absorb noise, provide padding surface for comfortable walking and standing, keeps rooms cozy and warm

3.9 The cut or uncut loops that project above the backing of the carpet.

3.10 family room, for it typically has the most activity

3.11 focal point

3.12 yes

3.13 smaller

3.14 wider

3.15 subtle

3.16 darker

3.17 Any of the following: paneling, ceramic tile, brick, stone

3.18 to admit light and air

3.19 drapes

3.20 Curtains have pockets at the top through which the curtain rod is run. Drapes have pinch-pleats and are attached to the rod with hooks.

3.21 Priscilla

3.22 A shade is a continuous piece of material that is rolled up. Blinds are made of slats that can be directed at varying angles.

3.23 decorative, privacy, control noise and light, helps conserve energy

3.24 Any two of the following: increase visually the apparent space in a room, bring out the best features of a room, affects the quality and effect of color, enhances texture.

3.25 general or background; local or task lighting; accent or decorative

3.26 local or task

3.27 fluorescent

3.28 decorative or accent

## SECTION FOUR

4.1    yes

4.2    yes

4.3    because they are dull and lackluster compared to originals

4.4    Original graphic prints are works of art that artists create and print in a limited number of copies.

4.5    Any of the following: embroidery, needlepoint, tapestries

4.6    Mirrors can be a decorative piece because of their shape or frame and what they reflect can make them interesting.

4.7    bottom of the artwork should be slightly below eye level

4.8    lack of balance, draws the eye up and out of the room to the ceiling

4.9    Answers may vary: clock, lamps, fancy jewelry box, hand mirror, decorative coasters, fireplace tools, etc.

4.10   Answers may vary: vase, figurine, carvings, floral arrangement

4.11   the angle from which it will be viewed

4.12   one side of arrangement is equal to the other

4.13   the tallest

4.14   Adult check

4.15   Adult check

**SECTION FIVE**

5.1     the patterns used for making slipcovers are
        often the chair or sofa being covered rather
        than a paper pattern

5.2     allowances

5.3     "decorator fabrics"

5.4     wrinkles, stains or fading

5.5     Appliqué is a small piece or pieces of fabric
        applied as decorative trimming by hand or
        machine.

5.6     trapunto

5.7     Any order:

        a. throw

        b. flounced

        c. tailored

5.8     Adult check

## SECTION ONE

1.1 Answers will vary. Should include something about a warm welcome and the care and concern for the guests comfort.

1.2 A house is a shelter or a place to eat and sleep; a home is the center of family life.

1.3 Answers will vary. By showing genuine concern for the welfare of guests; it is the spirit of the people not the tangible objects in the home.

1.4 food

1.5 Any unplanned event. Answers will vary, such as: spilled food, broken dishes, uninvited guests, etc.

1.6 Answers must be in order.
   a. decide on a guest list
   b. decide on an invitation
   c. decide on the menu
   d. decide on decorations
   e. decide on activities or entertainment
   f. schedule all preparation activities; the "do aheads"

1.7 ten or less

1.8 stagger the invitation hours

1.9 yes

1.10 Themes

1.11 Answers will vary. Examples: birthday, Christmas, baby or bridal showers, etc.

1.12 Formal

1.13 In any order:
   a. type of party
   b. who you have invited
   c. number of guests you have invited

1.14 theme

1.15 Any of the following: grocery shopping, preparing some dishes, cleaning the house, decorating, setting the table, polishing silver, etc.

1.16 keep a journal of each party you have given

1.17 between five and eight PM.

1.18 10-12

1.19 because it is easier for the host to manage a smaller number when there is no maid to help serve the guests

1.20 Brunch is a combination of breakfast and lunch.

1.21 Answer will vary, but should include several main dishes such as eggs Benedict, crepes, souffles, meat dishes, pancakes, French bread, etc. along with special breads, fresh fruit, juice, hot coffee and tea.

1.22 True

1.23 True

1.24 False

1.25 True

1.26 False

1.27 Answers will vary: crib, stroller, high chair, car seat, etc.

1.28 5 - 20 dollars

1.29 Answers may vary: have guests bring a spice, favorite recipe or write down words of advice.

1.30 yes

1.31 Gifts that they can both use. Answers may vary, examples: linens for bed and bath, tools, plants, decorative accessories, games, photo albums, appliances.

1.32 Adult check

1.33 privacy and cleanliness

1.34 separate guest bedroom with its own bathroom

1.35 test it yourself by sleeping in it

1.36 two twin beds

1.37 Answers will vary. See list in text.

1.38 Answers will vary. See list in text.

1.39 Show them to their bedroom and bathroom. Tell them what they need to know about supplies and controls (temperature, lights, etc.).

1.40 False

1.41 False

1.42 False

1.43 courtesy, decorum

1.44 overnight stays, a meal, an occasion when you are the guest of honor

1.45 when you arrive

1.46 two hours after dinner

1.47 no

1.48 Adult check

**SECTION TWO**

2.1 ladies

2.2 between courses only

2.3 no, two to three bites

2.4 knife or piece of bread

2.5 the hostess starts to unfold her napkin

2.6 nothing, you tell the host about the spill

2.7 the same way it went in - spit on fork and place on edge of plate

2.8 yes, in casual setting or at home, or in private

2.9 work from the outside to the inside

2.10 across the top of the plate

2.11 Any order: too much carry-on luggage and seat-mates that are too talkative

2.12 consideration of fellow guests

2.13 in case of fire or other emergencies

2.14 cellular phone

2.15 Any order: who initiates the date, who controls the date, who pays

2.16 Answers will vary, for example: Sally should not cancel the previous date, that would be extremely impolite. Sally should politely explain to Barry why she cannot go out with him, but since she really likes Barry, she should mention she would love to go out another time.

2.17 Answers will vary, for example: Molly needs to gently tell Gary that she doesn't think she is the right person for him, but thank him for asking.

2.18 2-4 days

2.19 call and ask in person

2.20 day, time, activity, transportation, who is going to be there, what to wear, who is paying, curfew

2.21 Any order: She can ask Bill if he wants to go Dutch treat, when she accepts the invite or she can just take money with her in case she needs to cover her own expenses.

2.22 Answers may vary, for example: have him over for supper or pack a picnic lunch.

2.23 So there will not a be a long wait or possible failure to get into the restaurant at all that night.

2.24 the guy

2.25 15%

## SECTION THREE

3.1     Upright model with powered beater-brush head.

3.2     Any order: whisk broom and push broom

3.3     cotton, more absorbent

3.4     A squeegee is an implement edged with rubber for removing water from windows after washing.

3.5     dusting, from as high as you can reach and work downward

3.6     wipe with soft cloth or vacuum with small brush attachment

3.7     in the same direction as the grain

3.8     time

3.9     vacuuming

3.10    wipe one side vertically the other side horizontally

3.11    vinegar and baking soda

3.12    getting rid of smells in garbage disposal

3.13    lemon wedge, salt

3.14    Adult check

3.15    fifteen years or older

3.16    paint, shingles, stucco, aluminum or vinyl siding

3.17    False

3.18    it sticks when you try to open or shut it

3.19    to see if it is worn or has a build-up of soap scum on it, causing it to partially plug the flow of water from the faucet

3.20    the flapper is not blocking the flush valve, so water keeps filling the tank

3.21    vinegar

3.22    to open a clogged drain

3.23    Adult check

3.24    flying objects in the case of an accident can be seriously harmful

3.25    Any order: dashboard cover and vinyl treatment cleaner

3.26    weekly

3.27    newspaper, less apt to streak

3.28    wax

3.29    to keep rubber on window seals from cracking

3.30    Parent/Adult check

3.31    Any order: coolant, brake fluid, transmission fluid, power steering fluid, window cleaning solution

3.32    if the pedal stop is mushy or the pedal keeps going to the floor when you put your foot down on the pedal

3.33    wipe it off and stick back in

3.34    every 3,000 miles

3.35    1/2 inch

3.36    prevents electrical circuits from being completed

3.37    it will look dirty

3.38    needs new light bulb

3.39    Parent/Adult check

**SECTION ONE**

1.1     descriptive

1.2     False

1.3     Adult check

1.4     A resume is a concise history of your achievements, education and previous job experience and skills.

1.5     chronological

1.6     functional

1.7     combination

1.8     Adult check

1.9     questions about your education, early background, achievements, work experience

1.10     It will give you confidence for the interview.

1.11     Being late sends a negative impression to the interviewer, whereas, being on time helps you feel more relaxed and confident.

1.12     Answers may vary, looking for conservative.

1.13     These people often give their impressions to their supervisor, which could affect whether or not you get the job.

1.14     with a firm handshake, smile, pleasant attitude and look him/her in the eye

1.15     makes you appear unfriendly or distant or indicates that you have something to hide

1.16     confidence

1.17     yes

1.18     Teacher/Parent/Potential Employer Check

## SECTION TWO

2.1 descriptive

2.2 financial

2.3 combination

2.4 Any two of the following: get a job, put money in bank, place order by mail, get a Social Security number, get a driver's license, to apply for college, to enter a hospital, to file income tax return, apply for insurance.

2.5 Verifying

2.6 expandable folder

2.7 fireproof box

2.8 safe-deposit box

2.9 safe-deposit box

2.10 expandable folder

2.11 c.

2.12 a.

2.13 c.

2.14 b.

2.15 a.

2.16 a.

2.17 d.

2.18 d.

2.19 d.

2.20 b.

2.21 b.

2.22 a.

2.23 b.

2.24 d.

2.25 charge fees for services and by collecting interest on loans

2.26 d.

2.27 c.

2.28 b.

2.29 a.

2.30 b.

2.31 c.

2.32 a.

2.33 check

2.34 deposit slip

2.35 signature card

2.36 endorsed

2.37 payee

2.38 check register

2.39 overdrawn, overdraft

2.40 bank statement

2.41 reconciling

2.42 Any order: earn interest, safe, depositing and withdrawing money is easy

2.43 interest

2.44 $100,000

2.45 regular

2.46 certificate of deposits

2.47 money market

2.48 Any order: stocks, bonds, mutual funds

2.49 Adult check

2.50 Adult check

2.51 Adult check

2.52 age 65

2.53 Any order: pension, 401(k)

2.54 Any order: IRA, annuity

2.55 Either order:
a. You pay back the principal,
b. You pay a finance charge.

2.56 a summary of your financial history

2.57 credit

2.58 charge account at a store

2.59 pay the total bill within 30 days

2.60 bank

2.61 Is the item purchased appreciable? Is it an investment?

2.62 Answers may vary.
a. No, she is too busy to even use a VCR if she is working full-time and going to college as well. She is already finding it hard to get time for social or sports activities. A VCR would only complicate things.

b. No, her expenses exceed her income. She is borrowing $100 a month from her parents. She is absolutely overextended, yet buys impulsively. She could also cut down on her expenses by purchasing used furniture instead of renting it, or go without. This alone would almost eliminate the need to borrow from her parents.

   c. "Thanks, but no thanks, no place in my budget for another monthly payment and I have no time to even use a VCR right now. It simply would not be wise or practical to purchase it now."

2.63   saves you and your family from becoming penniless through property loss, ill-health or the death of wage earner

2.64   A claim is your request for payment from an insurance company and a premium is the annual amount you pay for insurance coverage.

2.65   it protects your personal assets in case the injured party sues you

2.66   True

2.67   False

2.68   True

2.69   a.  add up your total income

        b.  subtract your deductions

        c.  apply the tax rate to find your tax

        d.  subtract your withholding and other payments and credits

2.70   student loan

2.71   standard deduction

2.72   dependent is someone who is depending on someone or something else for aid, support, etc.

2.73   Form W-4

2.74   Form W-2

2.75   1040EZ

## SECTION THREE

3.1 A bill of sale is written evidence of the transfer of title from one party to another.

3.2 yes

3.3 Any order: detailed description of the item, date of transfer from seller to buyer, signature of both parties

3.4 sales contract

3.5 False

3.6 True

3.7 Each individual state determines its own laws of intestacy which can determine the distribution of the decedents assets.

3.8 safe-deposit box

3.9 Probate is the legal process that involves filing the decedents will, identifying and accounting assets, paying debts and death taxes and distributing the remainder as dictated by the terms of the will.

3.10 Any order: living trusts, joint tenancy, designated beneficiaries

3.11 A living will is a directive to medical personnel to withhold or withdraw life-support equipment if you are suffering from a terminal or irreversible illness and death is imminent.

3.12 durable power of attorney

3.13 read it carefully; look for 'red flag' warnings

3.14 protect you from being held liable

3.15 False

3.16 False

3.17 True

3.18 Any order: car loan, insurance, license and registration, gas and oil, repairs and tires

3.19 number of miles driven

3.20 Across:
   2. decedent
   3. living will
   4. will
   7. durable power of attorney
   9. license
   10. lease

Down:
   1. beneficiaries
   5. intestacy
   6. odometer
   8. probate

## SECTION ONE

1.1    True

1.2    False

1.3    False

1.4    True

1.5    False

1.6    b.

1.7    f.

1.8    d.

1.9    g.

1.10   e.

1.11   a.

1.12   f.

1.13   c.

1.14   e.

1.15   2, 3 (either answer)

1.16   birth to 6 months

1.17   3, 4 (either)

1.18   one-year old

1.19   birth to 6 months

1.20   1, 2, 3 (any one answer is correct)

1.21   6 to 12 months

1.22   3, 4

1.23   True

1.24   True

1.25   False

1.26   False

1.27   True

1.28   True

1.29   True

1.30   True

1.31   True

1.32   True

1.33   False

1.34   True

1.35   False

1.36   True

1.37   True

1.38   False

1.39   In solitary play, the child plays alone; he is interested in his own activities, his own toys. In parallel play, the child plays next to another child but not with him; children may be doing the same activity, for example, stacking blocks. In cooperative play, the child will cooperate and play with one or more children, sharing and taking turns.

1.40   feed them when they are hungry, hold and cuddle when they cry, change diapers when needed, sing to them, read to them

1.41   three-year old

1.42   four-year old

1.43   young school-age child

1.44   Answers may vary. The three-year old is starting to be interested in sharing with others. Sharing is an act of kindness and could and should be praised. Teaching Bible stories about kindness and helpfulness would be good. Also Galatians 5:22–23.

1.45   Answers may vary. Observe–never force the child. The two-year old is interested in being near others but not participate in activities with them. He is beginning to observe adults and others, but not ready to participate. Letting him observe the family say grace will help teach him the importance of God and prayer. Set an example.

1.46   Adult check. Observation one.

1.47   Adult check. Observation two.

**SECTION TWO**

2.1   head and back (either order)

2.2   gather all essential materials

2.3   with your elbow

2.4   face

2.5   Soft comfortable clothes with no irritating tags, seams, ruffles, collars, ribbons or lace. Clothes that are easy to put on and take off.

2.6   as soon as it becomes wet or soiled

2.7   gently lift the ankles

2.8   A barrier cream is a cream or ointment to protect the baby's skin from moisture.

2.9   breast-feeding and bottle-feeding, breast-feeding, See chart 'Benefits of Breast Milk.'

2.10  Weaning is the process where the child becomes accustomed to food other than its mother's milk.

2.11  to get out the air that has built up in her stomach

2.12  rice cereal

2.13  help development of hand-to-mouth coordination (or eye/hand)

2.14  about 16 hours a day

2.15  Adult check

2.16  let them play, provide bubble bath, bath toys, make hairdos out of shampoo

2.17  brush teeth, comb hair, wash hands and clean nails, blow his own nose

2.18  Food Guide Pyramid

2.19  small amounts or limited amounts, 2, 5, $3\frac{1}{2}$, $1\frac{1}{2}$, 6 oz.

2.20  Any order: parental instruction—boundaries and rules are set; nurture—control and reinforcement of this instruction; admonition—necessary correction or punishment

2.21  Because the child has a short memory and they won't remember why they are being punished if you wait too long.

2.22  private, gentleness

2.23  True

2.24  False

2.25  False

2.26  True

2.27  False

2.28  False

2.29  False

2.30  a.

2.31  b.

2.32  d.

2.33  Adult check

2.34  Adult check

2.35  To help develop their vocabulary, give them an appreciation for literature, widen their horizons, help communicate your love for them and demonstrate your interest in spending time with them.

2.36  Adult check

2.37  Any four of the following: relaxing, method of releasing feelings, stimulus to movement, comforts a sad child and calms down the restless child, teaches child about the world he lives in and people he knows, teach about the love of God and teach Bible stories. Also an outlet for child's creativity.

2.38  Art is a means of creative self-expression in a visual form.

2.39  Adult check

2.40  Adult check

2.41  Adult check, Observation three.

2.42  True

2.43  False

2.44  True

2.45  Adult check

## SECTION THREE

3.1 In any order:
   a. keep all medicine out of the reach of children

   b. use safety catch on medicine cabinet door

   c. keep medicine bottles tightly closed or use child safety lids (or child proof)

3.2 Any two of the following: remove rusty nails, remove or fix loose broken boards, install a locked gated fence around swimming pool, provide proper supervision around pool.

3.3 Any four of the following: doctor, Poison Control Center, hospital, pharmacy, ambulance, police, fire (or 911), friend or relative to call for help.

3.4 keep locked or remove doors

3.5 proper hand washing

3.6 Any six of the following: adhesive tape, absorbent cotton, adhesive dressings in assorted sizes and shapes, gauze bandages, small sharp scissors, tweezers, clinical thermometer, safety pins, wooden applicator sticks, burn ointment and antiseptic.

3.7 baking soda, or soap to reduce itching, ice for inflammation, acetaminophen for pain

3.8 Any order: insect (bee) stings, medication and food

3.9 flush the wound with warm soapy water and apply an antiseptic cream or ointment

3.10 ice

3.11 locate the source, apply direct pressure, elevate the wounded appendage and in extreme cases, put pressure on the supplying artery

3.12 toward the bridge of the nose

3.13 hold under cool water until stinging stops

3.14 The first degree burn it the least severe. The first layer of skin, the dermis is the only layer involved and will be red. There is some pain. The second degree burn involves both the first and second layers of skin, the dermis and the epidermis. It will be red, tender and blistered. There is a lot of pain. The third degree burn involves all three layers of skin. The skin is white or black. There is no pain because the nerve endings have been damaged.

3.15 With heat exhaustion the victim is pale and has damp skin and no elevated temperature. With heat stroke the victim has a high fever and red, dry skin, no sweating, rapid heart beat, lethargy. Heat stroke is a medical emergency.

3.16 It is the safest emetic you can use. It induces vomiting.

3.17 Flush out with cold water for 15 minutes. Turn head with burned eye down so you won't contaminate the other eye. Cover with a clean cloth and go the doctor.

3.18 have child lie on back, raise legs, use a cold compress, check pulse and breathing

3.19 blow the nose to dislodge it, when the object is visible remove it with tweezers

3.20 cold compress

3.21 viral

3.22 3-10

3.23 Head lice inject a small amount of saliva under the skin, this injection causes itching.

3.24 a contagious, epidemic form of acute conjunctivitis

3.25 wash hands, apply warm compresses and therapeutic ointment or drops

3.26 2-8

3.27 Communicable means a disorder can be transmitted from one person to another, or capable of being easily transmitted.

3.28 13-17 days

3.29 True

## SECTION FOUR

4.1 Any two of the following: good health, dependability, responsible, con fident, level-headed, loves children, maturity, self-assurance, good manners

4.2 authority, discipline

4.3 privacy, closets, personal

4.4 stages

4.5 families are different

4.6 Any order: you are not being paid to talk on the phone, parents might be trying to check in, interferes with quality of child care

4.7 Any order: pay, expected time period you will be baby-sitting, extra tasks required, transportation arrangements

4.8 False

4.9 Any order: meals and menus, medication, playtime, bedtime, bath time, discipline

4.10 Any three of the following: know where locks, alarms and extra keys are located, know where emergency supplies are, know how to use basic appliances, know how to adjust heat and air conditioning, know the habits and care of pets, locate emergency paths and procedures in case of fire, tornado, earthquake or other emergency

**SECTION ONE**

1.1    Answers may vary: they may be preoccupied with their own concerns, they don't have enough information about the situation, they don't understand the situation well enough to make a decision

1.2    Either order: frankness, communication

1.3    "I," "You," defensive

1.4    with prayer

1.5    advance notice of needs reduces conflict of time schedules

1.6    Answers may vary. Examples: sharing computer and phone time, control of television and selecting programs; respecting others desires for time alone

1.7    trust

1.8    take more responsibility for yourself and help out running the household

1.9    False

1.10   True

1.11   a. Relationship: The state of being related by kindred, affinity or other alliance.

b. KINDRED,

1. Relation by birth

2. Relation by marriage; affinity.

3. Relatives by blood or marriage, more properly the former. Thou shalt go unto my country and to my kindred. (Gen. 26).

4. Relation; suit; connection by kind.

AFFINITY,

1. The relation contracted by marriage, between a husband and his wife's kindred, and between a wife and her husband's kindred; in contradistinction from consanguinity or relation by blood. Solomon made affinity with Pharaoh.
(I Kings 3).

2. Agreement; relation; conformity; resemblance; connection; as, the affinity of sounds, of colors, or of languages.

ALLIANCE,

1. The relation or union between families, contracted by marriage.

2. The union between nations, contracted by compact, treaty or league.

3. treaty, league, or compact, which is the instrument of confederacy; sometimes perhaps the act of confederating.

4. Any union or connection of interests between persons, families, states or corporations; as, an alliance between church and state.

5. The persons or parties allied; as, men or states may secure any alliances in their power.

c. Answers will vary

1.12   Adult/parent Check

1.13   Answers will vary. Example: I am fearfully and wonderfully made in the image of God. God has given me talents and abilities that He plans to use in a special way. If I realize or develop my own assets, I won't be jealous of others.

1.14   bathroom, always leave it tidy and clean and limit the time you occupy it

1.15   ask permission first

1.16   never

1.17   knock and wait for permission to enter

1.18   Answers will vary: when someone is doing something harmful to themselves or others; is dangerous; is immoral or is against the law

1.19   broken

1.20   Adult check

1.21   Answers will vary: for their need to be needed and for your need to learn from them, their life experience, their knowledge of your parents

1.22   Titus 2:3-5, I Timothy 4:12-13.

1.23   Any order: patience, support, loving, caring

1.24   Adult check

## SECTION TWO

2.1 cry

2.2 girls, boys

2.3 trust, intimacies, activities

2.4 A peer is a person that is equal in rank, age, abilities and qualifications whereas a friend is a person, no matter the rank, age, abilities, or qualifications that you are attached to by feelings of affection or personal regard.

2.5 Answers may vary.
trustworthy –Proverbs 31:11, loyal –Revelation 2:10, involved –Proverbs 18:24, willing to challenge, rebuke or exhort –2 Timothy 4:2, provide accountability –Romans 14:12

2.6 Answers may vary.
speaking courteously to others even when they don't agree, don't gossip about them, consider other person's likes and dislikes, fears, moral standards, etc., give them room to be different (principle of individuality)

2.7 because they expose a flaw

2.8 *4 to 1 principle,* try not to give one criticism until you have given four compliments to this person

2.9 Adult/Teacher check

2.10 "Education comprehends all that series of instruction and discipline which is intended to enlighten the understanding, correct the temper and form the manners and habits of youth and fit them for usefulness in their future stations."

2.11 detached professionalism and personal friendship

2.12 Any three of the following: guide, role model, counselor, encourager, evaluator.

2.13 use what he learns to expand his knowledge, skills and quality of lives

2.14 respect

2.15 because everyone is a teacher to someone to some extent throughout their life

2.16 Adult/Teacher check

2.17 Answers may vary.
A business is a group of individuals who must work together as a team in a congenial, amiable atmosphere to keep the operations running smoothly.

2.18 please, respond, accommodate

2.19 Answers may vary: job performance, loyalty to place of business, ability to communicate with co-workers, agreeable manners

2.20 True

2.21 False

2.22 False

2.23 True

2.24 True

2.25 True

2.26 Adult check

**SECTION THREE**

3.1 Answers may vary.
he wept, prayed and fasted for the people (families) of the church

3.2 Answers may vary.
Sunday School lessons on Christian marriage and the home, retreats and seminars on home and family, regular messages on the home.

3.3 Answers may vary.
Encourage a vital relationship with God, strengthen husband/wife relationships, build family strength, equip parents to teach Christian values, develop relational strengths, make sure God's will is preached.

3.4 Answers may vary.
glorify God and minister to others

3.5 Jesus Christ

3.6 Adult check

3.7 Any order: Teaches proper doctrine, ministers to the family, evangelizes in community.

3.8 Any order: tithe, time, talents

3.9 Answers will vary.

**SECTION FOUR**

4.1 talking too much during the performance

4.2 semi-formal or formal

4.3 she was late

4.4 standing in the back or out in the foyer

4.5 no talking, no walking, no things

4.6 False

4.7 Answers may vary: kind and courteous, encouraging the players and fellow spectators

4.8 Answers may vary: kind and courteous, being a good sport, encouraging

4.9 Answers may vary: give the opponent a handshake and a sincere "you played well"

4.10 congratulations

4.11 Any two of the following,
Any order: arrive on time – leave at appropriate time – mingle

4.12 Answers may vary.
because showing off can become tiresome and annoying; your conversation can become insulting, insensitive and offensive

4.13 Answers may vary.
forget about yourself and concentrate on others' needs and comfort

4.14 Answers may vary.
flowers are always up, which is the way they grow

## SECTION FIVE

5.1 Adult check

5.2 Adult check

5.3 Answers will vary.

5.4 Any order: in person, face-to-face

5.5 love, care

5.6 as virgins

5.7 Any two of the following or look up their answers to see if they fit: Matthew 19:6a, 2 Timothy 2:22, 1 John 1:9, Hebrews 13:4

5.8 True

5.9 True

5.10 True

5.11 True

5.12 True

5.13 True

5.14 True

5.15 Any order: spiritual, physical, emotional, social, financial

5.16 1 Peter 3:7

5.17 covenant

5.18 stick out like porcupine quills, grow inward.

5.19 Matthew 19:6, Hebrews 13:4

5.20 Submission is considering the other person's needs before we consider our own. yes

5.21 forgiveness

5.22 True

5.23 True

5.24 True

5.25 False

5.26 False

5.27 Answers will vary.

5.28 Answers may vary.
family members, especially parents have insights gained through experience and observation that can help you make an informed decision.

5.29 Answers may vary.
God is interested in our life mate choice and can answer our prayers concerning our choice. Prayer will protect and help keep God's choice for you pure and holy.

5.30 Answers may vary.
To give his/her parents wisdom as they raise him/her, To cause his/her heart to be responsive to Christ, To guard him/her from irreparable mistakes.

5.31 Answers may vary.
God promises in His Word that if we ask in prayer, believing He will give us the desires of our hearts. Matthew 7:7, 21:22, Luke 11:9, John 14:13–14, James 1:6 and 1 John 5:14–15.

**SELF TEST 1**

1.01    g.   virtue

1.02    e.   godliness

1.03    a.   knowledge

1.04    c.   patience

1.05    d.   temperance

1.06    b.   brotherly kindness

1.07    f.   charity

1.08    salvation

1.09    Answers may vary. Example, gossip because the Bible addresses this issue specifically, I Cor. 6:8.

1.010    Answers may vary. Example, going to movies because the Bible does not address this issue specifically. It is a personal decision.

1.011    God's Word

1.012    Any of the following: heredity, environment, family size or status, religion, role models, where you live.

1.013    values: that which is desirable or worthy of esteem for its own sake; merit

1.014    character: the features and traits that form the apparent individual nature of a person; the account of the qualities of a person

1.015    personality: the sum total of the physical, mental, emotional and social characteristics of an individual

1.016    role model: a person who demonstrates or models certain roles of honorable or admirable behavior

1.017    Any one: Individuality: we are created in God's image, yet we are complex and unique. Self-government: teaches us to control ourselves concerning behavior and discipline. Christian character: teaches us to do everything we do to the best of our abilities and to honor God. Conscience: our conscience is our safe guide to do right and must be trained and filled with Godly thoughts.

1.018    Family and friends are constantly watching us as we demonstrate the Christian principles that govern our behavior and can see us as we let God control our lives. We can either be an encouragement to others or a stumbling block.

**SELF TEST 2**

2.01    King

2.02    health, hygiene

2.03    food pyramid

2.04    a well-balanced diet

2.05    plaque, cavities

2.06    cleanliness, gloss, shape

2.07    proper body alignment

2.08    False

2.09    True

2.010   False

2.011   False

2.012   True

2.013   False

2.014   True

2.015   False

2.016   <u>vitality:</u> exuberant physical strength or mental vigor: power to live or grow

2.017   <u>nutrients:</u> a nourishing substance; essential for good health are proteins, carbohydrates, fats and oils, mineral, vitamins and water

2.018   <u>cholesterol:</u> a natural waxy substance made by the body. Excess amounts build upon the walls of blood vessels and gradually narrows them

2.019   <u>antiperspirant:</u> any preparation for retarding perspiration

2.020   <u>pedicure:</u> professional care or treatment of the feet

2.021   c.  muscle flexibility

2.022   d.  aerobic endurance

2.023   b.  muscle endurance

2.024   a.  muscle strength

2.025   It takes a great amount of discipline to stay physically fit, therefore, the principle of self-government plays a vital part in maintaining good health.

2.026   At least two of the following: protects your muscles from being burned for energy, builds new muscle, burns fat, increases energy levels, improves cardiovascular fitness and reduces the risk of osteoporosis.

**SELF TEST 3**

3.01    Christ

3.02    charity

3.03    thoughtfulness, courtesy

3.04    Either order:
        a. speaking
        b. listening

3.05    Lord

3.06    the other person

3.07    positive, pleasant, tactful

3.08    practice

3.09    God's Word

3.010   communication: a system of sending and receiving messages

3.011   tactful: having a keen sense of what to say or do to avoid giving offense; skill in dealing with difficult or delicate situations

3.012   new food pyramid: the division of foods into 5 groups plus oils that indicate what foods and how many servings of each type of food we should eat to maintain a well-balanced diet. The original food pyramid replaced the four food groups

3.013   principle of individuality: we are created in God's image, yet we are complex and unique

3.014   hygiene: is a condition or practice conducive to the preservation of health, as cleanliness.

3.015   personality: the sum total of the physical, mental, emotional and social characteristics of an individual

3.016   temperance: entails the don'ts of life: self-control towards yourself

3.017   Any three: well groomed; considerate of others; knows how to handle yourself in any situation with humor, tact and laughter; creates a harmonious atmosphere; shows appreciation to others; broad culture and good listener; organizer; speak properly; hard worker; self-disciplined; exemplifies the "fruit of the Spirit"; open to others opinions as long as they don't contradict the Bible.

3.018   A thank-you note is needed when you have received a gift, when you have been an overnight guest or a guest at a party, or when you received a special favor.

3.019   Listen to every word spoken, and look into the person's eyes while they are speaking.

3.020   In introducing a man to a woman, say the woman's name first. Likewise, older before younger of the same sex, married before single of same age, most prominent first. Examples will vary.

**SELF TEST 1**

1.01   False

1.02   True

1.03   True

1.04   False

1.05   True

1.06   True

1.07   False

1.08   False

1.09   True

1.010  True

1.011  refrigerator

1.012  the juices evaporate and burn

1.013  nutrients

1.014  electric

1.015  rising

1.016  internal

1.017  Answers will vary. Some examples found in the reading are: Keep cords from hanging down, block electric sockets, lock up chemicals, keep knives and small appliances out of their reach.

1.018  toaster oven

1.019  stand mixer

1.020  coffee maker

1.021  whisk

1.022  (dry) measuring cups

1.023  measuring spoons

1.024  liquid measuring cups

1.025  cake pans

1.026  pie pan

1.027  double boiler

1.028  sauce pan

1.029  grapefruit knife

1.030  large spatula

1.031  rolling pin

1.032  colander

1.033  potato masher

1.034  tongs

1.035  wire rack

1.036  vegetable peeler

1.037  The equipment and cabinets are placed on two adjacent sides; when possible, the sink and the range are placed at right angles to one another. See illustrations below.

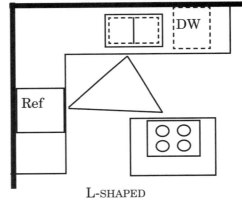

L-SHAPED

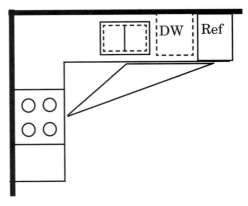

**SELF TEST 2**

2.01   List the ingredients in the order of their use.

2.02   Give exact measurements of all ingredients.

2.03   Include simple, step by step directions.

2.04   Give exact cooking time.

2.05   Give exact cooking temperature.

2.06   Tell size of utensil to use.

2.07   Give number and size of servings.

2.08   It should be a tested recipe.

2.09   c.  flour

2.010  f.  liquid

2.011  a.  eggs

2.012  d.  fats and oils

2.013  e.  leavening agent

2.014  g.  seasoning and flavoring

2.015  b.  sweetener

2.016  Spoon the ingredients lightly into a dry measuring cup and level with a straight-edge spatula or a knife.

2.017  Spoon ingredients into a dry measuring cup, pack down tight and level with a straight edge spatula or knife.

2.018  Pour into a measuring spoon until full

2.019  Pour the ingredient into a glass measuring cup and read the measurement at eye level while the cup is on a flat surface.

2.020  1 tablespoon

2.021  1/2 cup

2.022  8 fluid ounces

2.023  1 peck

2.024  1 pound

2.025  c.  fold

2.026  f.  fry

2.027  h.  strain

2.028  a.  baste

2.029  e.  whip

2.030  i.  toss

2.031  b.  cream

2.032  j.  mince

2.033  g.  grate

2.034  d.  mix

2.035  False

2.036  False

2.037  True

2.038  True

2.039  True

**SELF TEST 3**

3.01    plan menus and make a grocery list

3.02    avoid extras like cake, candy, soft drinks, low-nutrient snacks

3.03    raincheck

3.04    look for the "REAL" seal

3.05    during their peak growing season

3.06    The first item is most plentiful by % weight and the list continues in diminishing order down to the smallest quantity.

3.07    c.   chemical names for standard ingredients

3.08    a.   enriched

3.09    d.   one wall

3.010   c.   6 months–year

3.011   d.   blender

3.012   a.   flour

3.013   c.   12

3.014   b.   Blanch

3.015   b.   6 months

3.016   True

3.017   True

3.018   True

3.019   False

3.020   False

3.021   True

3.022   False

3.023   False

3.024   False

3.025   True

**SELF TEST 1**

1.01   a.   amino acids

1.02   f.   incomplete proteins

1.03   c.   complete proteins

1.04   e.   complex carbohydrates

1.05   g.   simple carbohydrates

1.06   h.   proteins

1.07   d.   fiber

1.08   b.   cholesterol

The following nutrients in any order:

1.09   proteins

1.010  carbohydrates

1.011  minerals

1.012  vitamins

1.013  fats

1.014  water

1.015  c.   Vitamin C

1.016  b.   Vitamin $B_1$

1.017  a.   Vitamin A

1.018  e.   Vitamin K

1.019  d.   Vitamin D

1.020  a.   Vitamin A

1.021  b.   Vitamin $B_1$

1.022  d.   fluoride

1.023  c.   iodine

1.024  a.   calcium

1.025  b.   iron

1.026  b.   6 (some LIFEPACs say 9)

1.027  d.   vitamins

1.028  c.   Vitamin C

1.029  c.   meat

1.030  b.   milk

1.031  c.   2 years

1.032  c.   anorexia nervosa

1.033  a.   malnutrition

1.034  i.   diabetes

1.035  d.   anemia

1.036  h.   rickets

1.037  b.   obesity

1.038  f.   night blindness

1.039  e.   goiter

1.040  g.   scurvy

**SELF TEST 2**

2.01    corn, rice

2.02    prepared, cooked

2.03    covered, uncovered

2.04    high, low

2.05    bones, teeth

2.06    gluten

2.07    b.  crispness

2.08    a.  2–4

2.09    c.  grown

2.010   b.  1/2

2.011   b.  age

2.012   c.  K

2.013   b.  fluorine

2.014   a.  air

2.015   c.  pastry

2.016   b.  provide tenderness, richness and flakiness

2.017   True

2.018   True

2.019   False

2.020   True

2.021   False

2.022   True

2.023   True

2.024   True

2.025   False

2.026   True

2.027   False

2.028   True

2.029   True

2.030   False

2.031   True

2.032   b.  stem

2.033   d.  seed

2.034   a.  root

2.035   c.  flower

2.036   e.  leafy

2.037   b.  tall bushes

2.038   d.  vines

2.039   c.  bushes

2.040   e.  close to the ground

2.041   a.  trees

2.042   Scalded milk is milk that has been heated until bubbles form a ring around the top.

2.043   Yogurt is a milk product low in fat, low in calories.

2.044   Marbling is the white streaks of fat running throughout the lean meat.

2.045   Aging of beef refers to the length of time beef cuts are stored under controlled temperatures and humidity before packaged for the meat counter.

2.046   A marinade is a savory liquid in which meats, fish, and vegetables are soaked before cooking.

2.047   Garnish are foods used to decorate food to make it more attractive.

2.048   b.  grade

2.049   e.  pan broil

2.050   a.  pan frying

2.051   d.  broiling

2.052   f.  braising

2.053   c.  roasting

2.054   c.  molded

2.055   d.  rolled

2.056   b.  refrigerator

2.057   e.  bar

2.058   a.  drop

2.059   f.  pressed

**SELF TEST 3**

3.01    main dish, protein

3.02    texture, flavor

3.03    season

3.04    need, appetites

3.05    appetizer, main course, dessert

3.06    True

3.07    True

3.08    False

3.09    True

3.010   True

3.011   False

3.012   False

3.013   True

3.014   False

3.015   True

3.016   True

3.017   The meal should <u>taste</u> good and incorporate at least 2 or 3 of the following tastes: sweet, sour, salty, bitter. The aroma (<u>smell</u>) of food cooking should be good. Bacon frying or popcorn popping appeals to the sense of <u>hearing</u>. Appropriate texture of foods, like smooth, creamy pudding satisfies the sense of <u>feeling</u>. Food should also be appealing to look at, <u>sight</u>.

**SELF TEST 4**

| | | | |
|---|---|---|---|
| 4.01 | formal, informal | 4.017 | True |
| 4.02 | English, Russian | 4.018 | True |
| 4.03 | Any two: simple or elaborate menu, time available for serving and eating, number of guests, the occasion | 4.019 | False |
| | | 4.020 | False |
| | | 4.021 | True |
| 4.04 | right | 4.022 | False |
| 4.05 | right | 4.023 | True |
| 4.06 | counterclockwise | 4.024 | True |
| 4.07 | left, right | 4.025 | True |
| 4.08 | e. English | 4.026 | True |
| 4.09 | b. buffet | 4.027 | False |
| 4.010 | c. family | 4.028 | False |
| 4.011 | f. Russian | 4.029 | True |
| 4.012 | a. blue plate | 4.030 | True |
| 4.013 | d. compromise | 4.031 | True |

4.014   <u>Demitasse</u> is a small cup of strong, dark coffee served after dinner.

4.032   See photo below.

4.015   <u>Table service</u> is the way or manner in which the foods are served at the table.

4.016   A <u>cover</u> is each person's place setting, including all the appointments he or she will need for the meal.

**SELF TEST 1**

| | | |
|---|---|---|
| 1.01 | | Protective |
| 1.02 | | True |
| 1.03 | | adornment |
| 1.04 | | Uniforms |
| 1.05 | | Status |
| 1.06 | | True |
| 1.07 | | True |
| 1.08 | | True |
| 1.09 | | bright and adventurous |
| 1.010 | | True |
| 1.011 | | True |
| 1.012 | h. | protection |
| 1.013 | e. | beauty |
| 1.014 | a. | identification |
| 1.015 | j. | dress code |
| 1.016 | c. | modesty |
| 1.017 | g. | conformity |
| 1.018 | i. | values |
| 1.019 | f. | personality |
| 1.020 | d. | attitudes |
| 1.021 | b. | status |

1.022  d.  camouflage suits, raincoats and bullet-proof vests

1.023  d.  decoration and beauty

1.024  d.  all of the above

1.025  c.  self-expression that distinguishes one person

1.026  c.  the direction in which fashion is moving

1.027  b.  enable a garment to fit the figure

1.028  a.  by a combination of the tailored and draped methods

1.029  d.  all of the above

1.030  b.  lower priced garment copies produced in volume

1.031  b.  the stock market

1.032  f.  fitted garments

1.033  d.  wardrobe

1.034  g.  tailored garments

1.035  e.  fad

1.036  b.  fashion

1.037  h.  apparel

1.038  a.  tubular silhouette

1.039  c.  classic

**SELF TEST 2**

2.01　a.　red, yellow, blue

2.02　c.　a temporary, passing fashion that dies quickly

2.03　a.　Hue

2.04　c.　complimentary

2.05　b.　sheath

2.06　a.　pleated

2.07　c.　palazzo

2.08　b.　batwing

2.09　e.　all of the above

2.010　c.　bateau

2.011　a.　mandarin

2.012　b.　dickey

2.013　c.　They should wear a complimentary color scheme.

2.014　a.　horizontal lines

2.015　d.　all of the above

2.016　a.　cool colors

2.017　c.　green

2.018　f.　cowl

2.019　b.　convertible

2.020　i.　knickers

2.021　e.　cardigan

2.022　g.　blazer

2.023　c.　bolero

2.024　a.　parka

2.025　j.　chesterfield

2.026　d.　Jabot

2.027　h.　blouson

2.028　True

2.029　False

2.030　True

2.031　True

2.032　False

2.033　True

2.034　True

2.035　False

2.036　True

2.037　True

2.038　<u>Draped</u> garments are those garments that are wrapped or hung on the body. (Ex. roman toga, poncho, or Indian sari). A <u>tailored</u> garment is one that is made by first cutting out pieces and then sewing them together to fit the shape of the body (Ex. jackets, pants, shirts). <u>Composite</u> garments are made by combining tailored and draped methods (Ex. kimonos, tunics, bathrobes, caftans, capes).

**SELF TEST 3**

3.01    <u>fiber production</u>: raw materials are processed into various fibers

3.02    <u>yarn production</u>: mills spin fibers into yarn

3.03    <u>fabric manufacturing</u>: plants weave or knit yarns into fabric

3.04    <u>fabric finishing</u>: finishing is done by bleaching, dying, printing or applying special coatings

3.05    from the puff protecting the seed of the cotton plant

3.06    from the stalk of the flax plant

3.07    from the fine filament from which the silk worm spins his cocoon

3.08    fleece of sheep

3.09    a.  cotton

       b.  linen

3.010   d.  wool

3.011   b.  linen

3.012   d.  wool

3.013   c.  silk

3.014   c.  silk

       d.  wool

3.015   a.  cotton

3.016   True

3.017   False

3.018   False

3.019   True

3.020   True

3.021   True

3.022   False

3.023   False

3.024   True

3.025   True

3.026   False

3.027   False

3.028   True

3.029   False

3.030   True

3.031   False

3.032   False

3.033   True

3.034   True

3.035   True

**SELF TEST 4**

4.01   d.   seam gauge

4.02   g.   thread

4.03   b.   scissors

4.04   e.   pinking shears

4.05   j.   beeswax

4.06   a.   safety pins

4.07   f.   thimble

4.08   h.   sewing machine

4.09   c.   fusible web

4.010   i.   seam ripper

4.011   b.   sharps

4.012   e.   all of the above

4.013   b.   removing cut threads

4.014   c.   sits on top of the buttonhole

4.015   c.   side seam

4.016   a.   backstitch

4.017   b.   blindstitch

4.018   b.   blindstitch

4.019   c.   catchstitch

4.020   d.   Wring out excess water on hand washed garments.

4.021   Any order:

a. color

b. fabric

c. bulk

d. amount of soil

4.022   60″

4.023   snaps

4.024   stretch

4.025   milk

4.026   cotton (or **preshrunk** linen)

4.027   delicate

**SELF TEST 1**

1.01    True

1.02    False

1.03    True

1.04    True

1.05    False

1.06    b.  feed dog

1.07    d.  presser foot

1.08    f.  stitch regulator

1.09    a.  bobbin

1.010   h.  throat plate

1.011   g.  tension regulator

1.012   c.  needle bar

1.013   h

1.014   g

1.015   j

1.016   e

1.017   i

1.018   b

1.019   a

1.020   d

1.021   c

1.022   f

**SELF TEST 2**

2.01    e.  even backstitch

2.02    c.  basting

2.03    k.  tailor tack

2.04    a.  backstitch

2.05    l.  topstitch

2.06    h.  outward curved seam

2.07    i.  inward curved seam

2.08    f.  flat-felled

2.09    d.  dart

2.010   j.  pleats

2.011   g.  gathering

2.012   a.  raveling

2.013   b.  5/8

2.014   b.  feed dogs

2.015   c.  grading

2.016   b.  tension regulator

2.017   b.  blanket stitch

2.018   b.  pinked

2.019   a.  throat plate

2.020   b.  bobbin

2.021   a.  neckline

2.022   c.  fly-front

2.023   bobbin

2.024   remove presser foot, attach special zipper foot

2.025   backstitch the wide end, sew off the edge at the point and tie the threads

2.026   In order as follows:
   a. measure and mark desired length.

   b. fold raw edge back 1/4″ - 1/2″ or finish edge using other methods. Press.

   c. fold back again to desired finished length.

   d. pin in place.

   e. stitch by hand or machine. Stitches should be neat, 1/8″ - 1/2″ apart and invisible on the right side. Press.

**SELF TEST 3**

3.01    b.  5/8

3.02    d.  overcast

3.03    c.  small print

3.04    a.  bias

3.05    a.  5

3.06    d.  1

3.07    c.  grain

3.08    c.  fillings

3.09    b.  interfacing

3.010   right

3.011   basting

3.012   notions

3.013   measurements

3.014   seam allowance

3.015   hand wheel or balance wheel

3.016   a

3.017   e

3.018   c

3.019   b

3.020   d

3.021   f

3.022   Any three of the following: pattern number, number of pattern pieces, pictures of pattern pieces, back views of pattern styles, garment descriptions, suggested fabric, notions needed, finished garment measurements, information on special fabrics, standard body measurements, yardage chart.

3.023   Any two of the following: pattern number, illustrations, pattern size, pattern company, price, special features (ex. "easy to sew" or "jiffy").

3.024   Any four of the following: name and number of pattern, pattern piece diagram, layout and cutting guide, alteration instructions, pattern markings, cutting and marking instructions, step-by-step sewing instructions.

**SELF TEST 4**

4.01    c

4.02    e

4.03    a

4.04    d

4.05    b

4.06    False

4.07    True

4.08    True

4.09    False

4.010   True

4.011   In any order:
    a. dots

    b. darts

    c. buttonholes

    d. placement lines for pockets and trims

4.012   In any order:
    a. raw edges meet

    b. selvages meet

    c. fold is flat

4.013   In any order:
    a. view number

    b. the size

    c. fabric width

4.014   Flattening a seam to make it smooth.

4.015   Third layer of fabric used for shaping the garment.

4.016   An extra seam added to give a detail or design look to the garment.

4.017   When the material has more than 1% shrinkage listed on the bolt.

**SELF TEST 1**

1.01    Louis XIV

1.02    Louis XV

1.03    Napoleon

1.04    German peasants

1.05    Hepplewhite

1.06    Duncan Phyfe

1.07    Shakers

1.08    Hitchcock

1.09    Federal

1.010   Breuer

1.011   False

1.012   False

1.013   True

1.014   True

1.015   True

1.016   excavation of Pompeii

1.017   wood or tile paneling reaching part-way up a wall, Spanish style

1.018   cabriole leg

1.019   Adams Brothers, Hepplewhite, Sheraton

1.020   The use of what seems best from various sources.

1.021   Two of the following: drop leaf table, table/chair combinations, storage chest bench

1.022   American Victorian style was more forbidding and used darker colors.

1.023   Furniture was made by machine, cheapening the quality. New materials were introduced, such as attached metal ornamentation rather than carved wood.

**SELF TEST 2**

2.01  Any order:
   a. red
   b. yellow
   c. blue

2.02  Any order:
   a. orange
   b. green
   c. purple

2.03  Any three of the following: color, line, texture, form, space

2.04  Any three of the following: proportion, scale, balance, rhythm, emphasis, unity

2.05  True

2.06  False

2.07  True

2.08  True

2.09  True

2.010 True

2.011 True

2.012 True

2.013 False

2.014 False

2.015 True

2.016 True

2.017 True

2.018 False

2.019 False

2.020 True

2.021 True

2.022 True

2.023 True

2.024 Furniture was made by machine, cheapening the quality. The introduction of new materials, such as metal for attached ornamentation instead of being carved.

**SELF TEST 3**

3.01   b.   cedar

3.02   b.   oak

3.03   b.   comes from trees that keep their leaves
            all year long

3.04   c.   vinyl tile

3.05   b.   family room

3.06   a.   red, blue, yellow

3.07   b.   intensity

3.08   b.   action, movement

3.09   c.   proportion

3.010  b.   floor plan

3.011  b.   American Revolution

3.012  b.   pinch-pleat

3.013  a.   shades

3.014  b.   Louis XV

3.015  b.   Hepplewhite

3.016  Any two of the following, any order: absorb
       noise, provide padding, warmth.

3.017  Any two of the following, any order: decora-
       tive, privacy, control noise and light, conserve
       energy.

3.018  Any two of the following: increase visually
       the amount of space in room, highlight the
       best feature or hide the worst, affects quality
       and effect of color, enhances texture.

3.019  True

3.020  False

3.021  True

3.022  True

3.023  True

3.024  True

3.025  True

3.026  False

3.027  True

3.028  False

**SELF TEST 4**

4.01    b.   The excavation of Pompeii

4.02    a.   Cabriole leg

4.03    c.   Better quality of furniture

4.04    b.   triadic

4.05    a.   traffic patterns

4.06    a.   proportion, balance, rhythm

4.07    c.   Mahogany, cherry, maple

4.08    c.   Artwork

4.09    a.   wool

4.010   d.   all of the above (the sun, the size of the
             room, personal finance)

4.011   True

4.012   False

4.013   True

4.014   False

4.015   False

4.016   True

4.017   True

4.018   True

4.019   False

4.020   True

**SELF TEST 1**

1.01   e.
1.02   g.
1.03   c.
1.04   b.
1.05   a.
1.06   f.
1.07   h.
1.08   d.
1.09   a.
1.010   d.
1.011   b.
1.012   c.
1.013   b.
1.014   a.
1.015   c.
1.016   b.

1.017   True
1.018   False
1.019   True

1.020   True
1.021   True
1.022   False
1.023   False
1.024   True
1.025   False
1.026   False

1.027   Answers may vary. Hospitality is the receiving and treating of guests and strangers in a warm, friendly, generous way.

1.028   Thermography is a process of writing or printing involving the use of heat. The lettering is raised.

1.029   Answers may vary. Our generous, warm spirit, administering comfort and concern for others is a mirror reflecting the image of Christ in our character.

**SELF TEST 2**

2.01    c.

2.02    c.

2.03    a.

2.04    a.

2.05    c.

2.06    b.

2.07    a.

2.08    c.

2.09    a.

2.010   True

2.011   False

2.012   True

2.013   True

2.014   False

2.015   False

2.016   True

2.017   True

2.018   Any order: oversized and/or too much carry-on luggage, too talkative

2.019   gentlemen

2.020   15%

2.021   Any order: privacy, cleanliness

2.022   Any order: who initiates the date, who controls the date, who pays

2.023   home

2.024   theme

2.025   10 or less

2.026   yes, Examples: what time he was picking her up,

what time he would be bringing her home (curfew?)

**SELF TEST 3**

| | |
|---|---|
| 3.01 | f. |
| 3.02 | e. |
| 3.03 | a. |
| 3.04 | b. |
| 3.05 | g. |
| 3.06 | d. |
| 3.07 | c. |
| 3.08 | False |
| 3.09 | True |
| 3.010 | True |
| 3.011 | False |
| 3.012 | True |
| 3.013 | True |
| 3.014 | True |
| 3.015 | False |
| 3.016 | True |
| 3.017 | False |
| 3.018 | True |
| 3.019 | True |
| 3.020 | True |
| 3.021 | False |
| 3.022 | True |
| 3.023 | False |

3.024　c.

3.025　b.

3.026　e.

3.027　a.

3.028　f.

3.029　d.

3.030　Any one of the following: clean closets, wash blankets, wash windows, clean screens, clean cabinets, wash stored dishes, wash walls.

3.031　possible injury from flying objects during an accident

3.032　Any four of the following: coolant, brakes and brake fluid, oil, transmission fluid, tires, power steering fluid, belts, battery, windshield wipers, air filter, external lights.

3.033　In order: turn off engine, pull dipstick out, clean dipstick off, reinsert dipstick and pull out again, notice the oil level (Full or Add). If level is between the two marks, it's okay. If the level is below the Add mark, then add oil.

**SELF TEST 1**

1.01    descriptive

1.02    chronological

1.03    functional

1.04    combination

1.05    conservatively

1.06    confidence

1.07    firm

1.08    False

1.09    True

1.010   False

1.011   True

1.012   True

1.013   False

1.014   True

1.015   True

1.016   False

1.017   True

1.018   A resume is a concise history of your achievements, education, and previous job experience.

1.019   Any two of the following: use general job titles, do not state current salary, keep to one page, must be typed.

1.020   Any order: education, achievements, work experience

1.021   Answers will vary. See text for guidelines.

**SELF TEST 2**

2.01    descriptive

2.02    financial

2.03    expandable folder

2.04    fire proof safe

2.05    safe-deposit box

2.06    a record book

2.07    a safe-deposit box

2.08    credit union

2.09    brokerage firm

2.010   pension

2.011   home loan

2.012   W-4

2.013   1040EZ

2.014   $100,000

2.015   b.

2.016   e.

2.017   f.

2.018   a.

2.019   g.

2.020   d.

2.021   h.

2.022   c.

2.023   True

2.024   False

2.025   False

2.026   True

2.027   True

2.028   True

2.029   True

2.030   True

2.031   A budget is a plan for using income to meet your needs and wants and to reach your goals.

2.032   Verifying is the process of checking information for completeness and accuracy.

2.033   Overdrawn is when check amount is greater than the account balance.

2.034   Reconciling is making the bank statement balance and check register balance agree.

2.035   from service charges and interest on loans

2.036   Any two of the following: loans, stocks, mutual funds.

2.037   Answers will vary. The first portion of your income should go to God/church. Be found faithful to God (1 Cor. 4.2), and He will meet your needs and sometimes even your wants. (Philippians 4:19).

2.038   In order:
   a. add up total income such as wages, interest and dividends

   b. subtract your deductions resulting in your taxable income

   c. apply the tax rates to find your tax

   d. subtract your withholding and other payments and credits: results in the amount of tax you owe, or the refund you have coming

**SELF TEST 3**

| | | | |
|---|---|---|---|
| 3.01 | False | 3.016 | Any order: detailed description of item, date of transfer, signature of both parties |
| 3.02 | True | 3.017 | safe-deposit box |
| 3.03 | True | 3.018 | joint-tenancy |
| 3.04 | False | 3.019 | durable power of attorney |
| 3.05 | False | 3.020 | beneficiaries |
| 3.06 | True | 3.021 | financial |
| 3.07 | True | 3.022 | achievements |
| 3.08 | True | 3.023 | brokerage firm |
| 3.09 | False | 3.024 | Probate is the official proving of a will as authentic or valid in a court |
| 3.010 | False | | |
| 3.011 | True | 3.025 | A lease is a contract renting land, property to another for a specified period of time and payment. |
| 3.012 | False | | |
| 3.013 | True | | |
| 3.014 | False | 3.026 | Any order: car loan, insurance, license and registration, gas and oil, repairs and tires |
| 3.015 | True | | |

**SELF TEST 1**

1.01    True

1.02    True

1.03    True

1.04    False

1.05    False

1.06    True

1.07    True

1.08    False

1.09    True

1.010    False

1.011    a.

1.012    d.  (Also c., see pg. 8)

1.013    c.

1.014    a.

1.015    b.

1.016    b.  (Or c. preschooler; see pg. 3)

1.017    d.

1.018    Any order: intellectual, emotional, spiritual

1.019    Any order: weight, motor skills

1.020    Any two of the following: God made me, God listens to me, God is with me, God can do all things, God loves me, He is my best friend.

1.021    Answers will vary. Example: Every child is a unique individual and will grow at a different rate and will learn at a different rate. Even with these individual differences, children of the same age are similar in their development.

**SELF TEST 2**

2.01    True

2.02    True

2.03    rice cereal

2.04    True

2.05    still needs

2.06    True

2.07    toddler

2.08    3-5

2.09    True

2.010   True

2.011   automatically receive

2.012   back, neck or head

2.013   hand to mouth (hand/eye)

2.014   Food Pyramid

2.015   d.

2.016   a.

2.017   c.

2.018   f.

2.019   Any four of the following:
        In any order: matter and energy, living things and their activities, our earth and the universe, man and his environment.

2.020   Any four of the following:
        In any order: relaxing, method of releasing feelings, stimulus to movement, comforts the sad child or calms down the restless child, teaches child about the world he lives in and people he knows, teaches the love of God and Bible stories taught through the lyrics, provides a creative outlet for the child.

2.021   Any three of the following:
        In any order: crayons, soap paint, tempera paint, finger paint, clay, playdough, collage, cutting and pasting.

2.022   Music is a combination of tones or a rhythmic sequence of pleasing sound.

2.023   Adventure play is the overcoming of obstacles: climbing, jumping, crawling, balancing.

**SELF TEST 3**

3.01   False

3.02   False

3.03   True

3.04   True

3.05   False

3.06   True

3.07   False

3.08   True

3.09   True

3.010  True

3.011  1, 38

3.012  insect (bee) stings

3.013  direct pressure, elevate

3.014  stop, drop, roll

3.015  syrup of ipecac

3.016  a.  The first-degree burn it the least severe. The first layer of skin, the dermis is the only layer involved and will be red. There is some pain.

   b.  The second-degree burn involves both the first and second layers of skin, the dermis and the epidermis. It will be red, tender and blistered. There is a lot of pain.

   c.  The third-degree burn involves all three layers of skin. The skin is white or black. There is no pain because the nerve endings have been damaged. Seek medical help.

3.017  With heat exhaustion the victim has pale, damp skin and no elevated temperature. With heat stroke the victim has a high fever and red, dry skin, no sweating rapid heartbeat, lethargy.

3.018  Any order: pink eye, chicken pox, head lice

3.019  wash with warm soapy water, apply antiseptic, bandage

3.020  flush with water in the direction away from the non-affected eye for about 15 minutes; cover with clean cloth and go to the doctor, find out the name of the chemical

3.021  have the child lay down, elevate feet, and apply a cool cloth to forehead, check pulse

**SELF TEST 4**

4.01   a.

4.02   d.

4.03   c.

4.04   c.

4.05   2 1/2

4.06   support back and head

4.07   read to them

4.08   Any three:
In any order: pay, expected time period you will be babysitting, extra tasks required; i.e., wash dishes, house cleaning, transportation arrangements.

4.09   Any three of the following:
In any order: good health, dependable, responsible, loves children, mature, level-headed, self-confident, knowledgeable of children, respectful of privacy.

4.010  Answers will vary.
Examples are: never leave child unattended, be aware of safe toys for particular ages, be aware of and pick up outside dangers, be alert to strangers, know emergency procedures and exit paths.

4.011  Any two of the following:
In any order: meals and menus, medication, playtime, bedtime, bath time, discipline.

4.012  Answers will vary.
Examples: don't socialize, play with the child, be kind but firm, comfort the crying child, make mealtime pleasant, follow bedtime routine, keep safe.

**SELF TEST 1**

1.01   Answers may vary: Relationship is the state of being related by kindred, affinity, or other alliance.

1.02   In order:

a. prayer

b. Find out how each person involved feels.

c. Lay out the facts.

d. Work on a solution.

e. Ask for forgiveness when necessary.

f. prayer

1.03   Any two of the following: ask permission first, return promptly, return item in same condition as when it was loaned to you, replace or repair if broken.

1.04   b.

1.05   a.

1.06   a.

1.07   a.

1.08   False

1.09   True

1.010  False

1.011  True

1.012  False

1.013  True

1.014  True

1.015  Answers may vary: communication–advance notice of need for use and get permission; cooperation–willing to help with maintenance, running errands and transportation for younger siblings; organization–plan your needs to incorporate both communication and cooperation.

**SELF TEST 2**

2.01    In this order: instruction, discipline, enlighten, understanding, temper, usefulness

2.02    False

2.03    True

2.04    True

2.05    True

2.06    False

2.07    True

2.08    True

2.09    False

2.010   Answers will vary.

2.011   Don't give criticism to another person until you have given four compliments to that person first.

2.012   Answers may vary.
        A peer is a person that is equal in rank, age, abilities, or qualifications. A friend is a person no matter the rank, age, abilities, or qualifications that is attached to another by feelings of affection or personal regard.

2.013   a.

2.014   c.

2.015   b.

2.016   b.

2.017   c.

2.018   a.

2.019   a.

2.020   Answers may vary.
        A competent teacher knows the subject. A trustworthy teacher promotes positive student relationships; has the welfare of the students in mind. A dynamic teacher loves teaching and uses a variety of skills in presentation.

**SELF TEST 3**

3.01    Nehemiah

3.02    True

3.03    talents

3.04    peer

3.05    True

3.06    general workforce

3.07    God, minister to others

3.08    doctrines, evangelizes

3.09    Either order: communication, organization

3.010   professionalism, friendship

3.011   Answers may vary.
         Sunday school lessons on Christian marriage and the home, retreats and seminars on home and family, regular messages on the home.

3.012   Any three of the following, any order: encourage a vital relationship with God, strengthen the husband/wife relationship, build family strength, equip parents to teach Christian values, develop relational strengths.

## SELF TEST 4

4.01   True

4.02   True

4.03   False

4.04   True

4.05   False

4.06   True

4.07   True

4.08   True

4.09   False

4.010  True

4.011  True

4.012  True

4.013  You will either rudely disturb others while finding your seat, or you will have to stand in the back or out in the hall until intermission, possibly missing the first part of the performance.

4.014  clap

4.015  Answers may vary.
       be kind and courteous throughout play, shake opponents hand whether you win or lose, congratulate the winner with sincerity

4.016  Answers may vary.
       forget about yourself, concentrate on the needs and comforts of others

**SELF TEST 5**

5.01    because it is a strong indication of how they will treat you

5.02    Answers may vary: but should say something about reflecting on his/her treatment of you. Children emulate what they see in their own parents and family. Sometimes, as adults they don't realize there is any other way to act. To them it is normal to abuse.

5.03    Answers may vary: you can become too involved, become too intimate, pressure from being turned down when asking someone to go out.

5.04    You marry more than just the individual. You marry their whole family, friends, and church.

5.05    b.

5.06    d.

5.07    a.

5.08    c.

5.09    a.

5.010   b.

5.011   a.

5.012   c.

5.013   Answers may vary.
        God is interested in our life mate choice and can answer our prayers concerning our choice. Prayer will help protect and help keep God's choice for you pure and holy. Proverbs. 8:17. Pray that God will give his/her parents wisdom as they raise him/her; to cause his/her heart to be responsive to Christ and to guard him/her from irreparable mistakes. God promises in His Word that if we ask in prayer believing, He will give us the desires of our hearts — Matthew 7:7, 21:22, Luke 11:9, John 14:13–14, James 1:6, 1 John 5:14–15.

**Test Key**

1. a. self-government
2. d. conscience
3. c. individuality
4. a. self-government
5. b. Christian character
6. <u>virtue:</u> moral excellence; goodness, righteousness
7. <u>patience:</u> bearing provocation, annoyance, pain
8. <u>brotherly kindness:</u> right actions or attitudes towards other Christians
9. <u>nutrition:</u> the process by which plants and animals take in and use food materials
10. <u>astringent:</u> a cosmetic that cleans the skin and constricts the pores
11. <u>manicure:</u> treatment of the hands and fingernails for removing cuticle, trimming and shaping nails
12. b. homosexuality
13. b. temperament and character
14. c. grains
15. a. aerobic endurance
16. c. oval
17. c. eyes
18. a. good body alignment
19. a. speaking and listening
20. b. "Grandma, may I introduce my friend Sally."

21. True
22. True
23. False
24. True
25. False
26. True
27. True
28. False
29. False
30. False
31. True
32. False
33. False
34. True
35. It takes a great amount of discipline to stay physically fit.
36. Answers will vary
37. Biblical principles are those principles based on Scripture and are never changing. Personal preferences change from generation to generation, culture to culture and day to day. Personal preferences are not addressed by the Scriptures in a clear or definite manner.
38. Health is a state of wellness, and hygiene is the method or technique for maintaining that state of wellness.

**Test Key**

| | | | | | |
|---|---|---|---|---|---|
| 1. | e. | whip | 31. | | whisk |
| 2. | f. | dice | 32. | | paring knife |
| 3. | a. | simmer | 33. | | basting brushes |
| 4. | b. | blend | 34. | | tongs |
| 5. | c. | mix | 35. | | measuring spoons |
| 6. | h. | baste | 36. | | cooling rack |
| 7. | e. | pan broil | 37. | | measuring cups (dry ingredients) |
| 8. | d. | dry ingredients | 38. | | vegetable peeler |
| 9. | b. | one tablespoon | 39. | | grater |
| 10. | g. | simmer | 40. | | colander |
| 11. | a. | one cup | 41. | | liquid measuring cups |

1.  e.  whip
2.  f.  dice
3.  a.  simmer
4.  b.  blend
5.  c.  mix
6.  h.  baste
7.  e.  pan broil
8.  d.  dry ingredients
9.  b.  one tablespoon
10. g.  simmer
11. a.  one cup
12. c.  recipes
13. f.  sauté
14. d.  stand mixer
15. f.  blender
16. g.  crock pot
17. a.  frying pan
18. c.  hand mixer
19. e.  paring knife
20. b.  can opener
21. False
22. True
23. True
24. False
25. True
26. False
27. True
28. True
29. large spatula
30. rolling pin

31. whisk
32. paring knife
33. basting brushes
34. tongs
35. measuring spoons
36. cooling rack
37. measuring cups (dry ingredients)
38. vegetable peeler
39. grater
40. colander
41. liquid measuring cups

(42.- 47. Can be given in any order. *Note:* Listing knife size is optional.)

42. 3″ paring knife
43. 5″ or 6″ utility knife
44. 8″ or 9″ steak and poultry knife
45. a 9″ roast slicer
46. 8″ or 10″ French cook's or chef's knife
47. serrated edge bread and cake knife

(48. - 49. Can be any two of the following.)

    a.  front of the can has pictures or words that show what to expect inside the can
    b.  tells how to serve
    c.  tells how many servings
    d.  gives directions for preparation
    e.  nutritional information
    f.  weight of product
    g.  ingredients
    h.  number of calories, number of calories from fat
    i.  special diet information

**Test Key**

1.  a.  2–3
2.  c.  meats, eggs, cheese and fish
3.  a.  citrus fruits and leafy vegetables
4.  c.  milk/dairy products
5.  d.  all of the above
6.  c.  Vitamin D
7.  c.  liver
8.  b.  6–8
9.  a.  green and yellow vegetables
10. b.  Vitamin C
11. e.  Vitamin A
12. a.  calcium
13. g.  Vitamin D
14. d.  iron
15. c.  iodine
16. f.  Vitamin B
17. False
18. True
19. True
20. False
21. True
22. True
23. True
24. True
25. True
26. False
27. True
28. True
29. True

30. True
31. True
32. True
33. True
34. False
35. True
36. grown
37. Air
38. fat

39. starch
40. roasting
41. five senses
42. Russian
43. animal
44. growth, maintenance
45. Any two: growth, women breast feeding, health, stature, weight, size, activity, age
46. 1/2
47. prime
48. marbling
49. dessert
50. <u>Trace minerals</u> are minerals that are found only in small amounts in the body.
51. <u>Marinating</u> is the process of placing meat, fish, or vegetables in a liquid for several hours to enhance flavor and tenderize before cooking.
52. A <u>cover</u> is each person's place setting, including all of the appointments she or he will need for the meal.

**Test Key**

| | | |
|---|---|---|
| 1. | l. | nylon |
| 2. | f. | dart |
| 3. | i. | haute couture |
| 4. | j. | knock-offs |
| 5. | c. | bodice |
| 6. | q. | value |
| 7. | m. | personality |
| 8. | a. | attitude |
| 9. | o. | pleated |
| 10. | k. | mandarin |
| 11. | e. | cowl |
| 12. | d. | bolero |
| 13. | n. | Peter Pan |
| 14. | g. | gored |
| 15. | p. | princess |
| 16. | h. | empire |
| 17. | b. | bateau |
| 18. | a. | horizontal lines or stripes |
| 19. | b. | longer skirt hemlines |
| 20. | c. | tailored garments |
| 21. | b. | fashion |
| 22. | d. | all of the above |
| 23. | a. | hue |
| 24. | c. | complimentary |
| 25. | d. | both a. (color and fabric) and b. (bulk and amount) |
| 26. | d. | both a. (60″ long) and c. (5' long) |
| 27. | b. | milk |
| 28. | c. | finishing seams and raw edges |
| 29. | a. | cotton |
| | b. | linen |

| | | |
|---|---|---|
| 30. | g. | acrylic |
| 31. | d. | wool |
| 32. | e. | polyester |
| 33. | b. | linen |
| 34. | d. | wool |
| 35. | b. | linen |
| 36. | f. | Orlon |
| 37. | c. | silk |
| | d. | wool |
| 38. | a. | cotton |
| 39. | | True |
| 40. | | False |
| 41. | | True |
| 42. | | True |
| 43. | | False |
| 44. | | True |
| 45. | | True |
| 46. | | False |
| 47. | | True |
| 48. | | False |
| 49. | | True |
| 50. | | True |
| 51. | | False |
| 52. | | True |
| 53. | | True |
| 54. | a. | increases your size |
| 55. | b. | decreases your size |
| 56. | a. | increases your size |
| 57. | a. | increases your size |
| 58. | a. | increases your size |

## Test Key

1.   o.   woof
2.   j.   preshrinking
3.   n.   warp
4.   i.   plaids and stripes
5.   b.   cotton
6.   g.   nylon
7.   a.   basting stitch
8.   l.   seams
9.   f.   facings
10.  m.   allowance
11.  c.   darts
12.  e.   "Easy to make" patterns
13.  k.   pressing
14.  h.   pattern guide sheet
15.  d.   wrong side
16.  False
17.  True
18.  True
19.  False
20.  True
21.  True
22.  True
23.  b.   bias
24.  a.   Nap

25.  b.   blanket stitch
26.  a.   Fillings
27.  c.   Interfacing
28.  b.   grading
29.  lengthwise
30.  one
31.  Yes, because each pattern piece grain line indicates each piece to be laid on the lengthwise grain.
32.  c.
33.  d.
34.  e.
35.  f.
36.  a.
37.  cut the pattern in two at alteration line, then separate it evenly onto tissue paper
38.  Any two of the following: hangs parallel to the floor, stitches do not show on outside, clean finished raw edge, should appear flat and smooth from outside.
39.  A guide sheet is the sheet of paper inside the pattern envelope that gives the name and number of the pattern, piece diagram, cutting guides, alteration instructions, pattern markings, cutting and marking instructions and step-by-step sewing instructions.

**Test Key**

1.  c.  Empire
2.  e.  Rocking chair
3.  g.  Wainscot
4.  f.  Shield-back
5.  d.  International style
6.  b.  Baroque
7.  a.  Art Nouveau
8.  False
9.  True
10. True
11. False
12. False
13. True
14. False
15. False
16. True
17. True
18. False
19. False
20. True
21. False
22. True
23. True
24. c.  templates
25. e.  traffic patterns
26. a.  floor plan

27. d.  extended analogous
28. f.  triad
29. b.  orange, green, purple
30. b.  action, movement
31. c.  vinyl tile
32. a.  scale
33. a.  American Revolution
34. a.  shades
35. b.  Excavation of Pompeii
36. c.  Mahogany, cherry, ample
37. b.  Lamp
38. c.  Acrylic
39. a.  Ceiling, wall, floor
40. a.  Makes a room look larger
41. b.  Makes a room look smaller
42. a.  larger
43. b.  smaller
44. b.  smaller
45. a.  larger
46. allowances
47. Small pieces of fabric applied as decorative trimming by hand or machine.
48. Furniture was made by machine, cheapening quality; and the introduction of new materials for attached ornamentation rather than being carved.

**Test Key**

1.  c. Food
2.  a. home
3.  a. privacy and cleanliness
4.  b. try it yourself
5.  c. Who initiates the date, who controls the date, who pays
6.  b. Be honest (See LP)
7.  c. either a or b
8.  a. 15%
9.  b. Excuse himself, go to the restroom and remove it.
10. b. call the manager
11. a. dust
12. b. 3,000 miles
13. Hospitality is the receiving and treating of guests and strangers in a warm, friendly, generous way.
14. True
15. True
16. False
17. True
18. False
19. True
20. True
21. False
22. True
23. False
24. True
25. True
26. True
27. True
28. True
29. True
30. False
31. False
32. False
33. True
34. In Order (Make sure the student has the significant steps)

  a. Park on a level surface, activate hazard flashers and set the parking brake.

  b. Place gearshift lever in P (Park).

  c. Block the diagonally opposite wheel.

  d. Use the tip of the lug wrench to remove any wheel trim (hub cap, etc.).

  e. Loosen each wheel lug nut, but do not remove them until the wheel is raised up off the ground.

  f. Position the jack according to the directions. Turn the jack handle clockwise until the tire is raised approximately 1″ off the ground.

  g. Remove the lug nuts with the lug wrench. Replace the flat tire with the spare tire.

  h. Reinstall the lug nuts, cone side in, until the wheel is snug against the hub. Do not fully tighten the lug nuts until the wheel has been lowered.

  i. Lower the wheel by turning the jack handle counterclockwise.

  j. Remove the jack and full tighten the lug nuts.

  k. Replace all wheel trim.

**Test Key**

1.  a.
2.  b.
3.  c.
4.  c.
5.  a.
6.  b.
7.  c.
8.  a.
9.  b.
10. a.
11. c.
12. a.
13. b.
14. c.
15. a.
16. b.
17. c.
18. b.
19. a.
20. c.

21. Answers will vary. Should discuss the following: showing interest, alertness, and guards against the interviewer assuming you have something to hide or you are not friendly.

22. Answers will vary. See text. Need to have more than just conservative. Could include color, style, accessories, etc.

23. Answers will vary.

**Test Key**

1. b.
2. b. *or* c.
3. a.
4. d.
5. c.
6. a.
7. f.
8. d.
9. b.
10. e.
11. e.
12. d.
13. a.
14. c.
15. f.
16. Answers will vary: God made all good things, God loves me, God listens to me, God sees me, God can do all things.
17. True
18. False
19. True
20. True
21. True
22. False
23. False
24. True
25. True
26. True
27. True
28. False
29. False
30. True
31. back and head (either order)
32. hand-to-mouth (or hand/eye)
33. nurture, admonition (either order)
34. chicken pox, head lice, pink eye (any order)
35. direct pressure, elevate
36. Answers will vary. Make sure answers include some of the following:

    self-confident, mature, likes and enjoys children, flexible, level-headed, calm, courteous, respectful of privacy, professional and businesslike

**Test Key**

1.  a. and b., either answer
2.  c.
3.  a.
4.  b.
5.  c.
6.  False
7.  True
8.  False
9.  True
10. True
11. True
12. False
13. False
14. False
15. True
16. True
17. False
18. True
19. True
20. True
21. "I," "you," defensive
22. *4 to 1*
23. competent, trustworthy, dynamic
24. ask permission first
25. Any two of the following: trustworthy, loyal, involved, respectful, accountability to each other, exhorts, etc.
26. Any two of the following: encourages a vital relationship with God, strengthen husband/wife relationship, builds family strength, equips parents to teach Christian values, develops relational strengths.
27. Any order: tithes, time, talents
28. Is he/she a Christian?
29. Submission
30. Answers will vary.

**Alternate Test Key**

1. g. virtue
2. a. knowledge
3. d. temperance
4. f. charity
5. e. godliness
6. c. patience
7. b. brotherly kindness
8. a
9. b
10. a
11. b
12. a
13. b
14. e. fat
15. d. sugar
16. c. eating too little
17. b. salt
18. a. carbohydrates
19. at least once a day
20. moisture given off by the body combined with any body dirt or soiled clothing and warmed by the skin
21. oval
22. the eyes
23. proper body alignment
24. the food pyramid
25. a well-balanced diet
26. words like thank-you, please, pardon me
27. c. muscle flexibility
28. d. aerobic endurance
29. b. muscle endurance
30. a. muscle strength
31. Personality is the sum total of the physical, mental, emotional and social characteristics of an individual.

32. Nutrients are a nourishing substance; essential for good health are proteins, carbohydrates, fats and oils, minerals, vitamins and water.
33. An antiperspirant is any preparation for retarding perspiration.
34. A manicure is a treatment of the hands and nails for the removing of cuticle, trimming and shaping nails.
35. Carriage is the manner of carrying the head and body; bearing.
36. Communication is a system for sending and receiving messages.
37. Any one: Individuality: we are created in God's image, yet we are complex and unique. Self-government: teaches us to control ourselves concerning behavior and discipline. Christian character: teaches us to do everything we do to the best of our abilities and to honor God. Conscience: our conscience is our safe guide to do right and must be trained and filled with Godly thoughts.
38. Health is a state of wellness and hygiene is the method or technique for maintaining that state of wellness.
39. Aerobics protect your muscles from being burned for energy and builds new muscle, which burns fat, increases your energy level, improves cardiovascular fitness and reduces the risk of osteoporosis.
40. Wash once or twice daily with a gentle, creamy soap or cleanser that moisturizes your face as it removes dirt; with upward strokes apply moisturizing cream to face twice daily; use a mask for dry skin once or twice a month; use a humidifier during the dry season.
41. "Mother, This is my friend Katie. Katie, this is my mother."

**Alternate Test Key**

| | | | | |
|---|---|---|---|---|
| 1. | True | 25. | c. | waffle iron |
| 2. | False | 26. | f. | bread machine |
| 3. | False | 27. | b. | blender |
| 4. | True | 28. | g. | electric fry pan |
| 5. | True | 29. | e. | toaster oven |
| 6. | True | 30. | a. | crock pot |
| 7. | False | 31. | d. | toaster |
| 8. | False | 32. | e. | sweetener |
| 9. | False | 33. | b. | flour |
| 10. | False | 34. | f. | seasoning |
| 11. | True | 35. | d. | leavening agent |
| 12. | False | 36. | a. | eggs |
| 13. | True | 37. | c. | fat |
| 14. | False | 38. | e. | chop |
| 15. | True | 39. | b. | whip |
| 16. | True | 40. | h. | roast |
| 17. | True | 41. | a. | fold |
| 18. | False | 42. | d. | simmer |
| 19. | True | 43. | f. | dice |
| 20. | True | 44. | c. | braise |
| 21. | False | 45. | g. | knead |
| 22. | False | | | |
| 23. | True | | | |
| 24. | False | | | |

## Alternate Test Key

1.  False
2.  True
3.  True
4.  False
5.  False
6.  True
7.  True
8.  False
9.  True
10. True
11. True
12. False
13. True
14. False
15. False
16. True
17. True
18. True
19. True
20. False
21. False
22. True
23. True
24. False
25. False
26. False

27. True
28. False
29. True
30. True
31. Bread, Cereal, Rice and Pasta: 4–10 servings (some LIFEPACs say 6-11 servings)

    Fruits: 2–4 servings

    Vegetables: 3–5 servings

    Meat, Poultry, Fish, Dry Beans, Egg and Nuts: 2–3 servings

    Milk, Yogurt and Cheese: 2–3 servings

    Fats, Oils and Sweets: use sparingly

32. A good pastry crust should be golden brown in color, have blistery surface and uniform, attractive edges. It should cut easily with a table knife but hold its shape when served. It should have a flaky texture and crispy rim. The flavor should be pleasant, but bland to enhance the flavor of the filling.

33. Answers will vary but should address each of the five senses. The meal should taste good and incorporate at least 2 or 3 of the following tastes: sweet, sour, salty, bitter. The aroma (smell) of food cooking should be good. Bacon frying or popcorn popping appeals to the sense of hearing. Appropriate texture of foods, like smooth creamy pudding satisfies the sense of feeling. Food should also be appealing to look at, sight.

34. See photo below.

**Alternate Test Key**

1. bulk
2. closed
3. cold water
4. delicate
5. wool
6. Cellulose
7. dress-code
8. protection
9. Status
10. analogous
11. Proportion
12. neutral
13. False
14. True
15. False
16. False
17. True
18. True
19. True
20. True
21. False

22. True
23. False
24. True
25. True
26. True
27. False
28. True
29. False
30. True
31. False
32. empire
33. dirndl
34. harem
35. cap
36. jewel
37. rolled
38. dickey
39. <u>Value</u> is an idea, belief or thing that is important to a person.
40. <u>Wardrobe</u> is all of the apparel a person owns.

**Alternate Test Key**

1.  True
2.  True
3.  False
4.  True
5.  False
6.  False
7.  True
8.  False
9.  True
10. True

11.  a.  alteration symbol
12.  i.  seam line symbol
13.  h.  seam allowance
14.  k.  top stitching
15.  b.  backstitch
16.  e.  facing
17.  j.  right
18.  m.  woof
19.  g.  pattern guide sheet or f. Mom
20.  c.  basting stitch

21.  Any order: raw edges meet, selvages meet, fold is flat
22.  Any order: what view you plan to use, what size and fabric width

## Alternate Test Key

1.  c.  Queen Anne
2.  g.  Hitchcock
3.  f.  Alvar Aalto
4.  a.  Louis XV
5.  d.  Victorian
6.  b.  German peasant
7.  e.  Shaker
8.  True
9.  True
10. False
11. True
12. False
13. True
14. False
15. True
16. True
17. True
18. True
19. True
20. False
21. True
22. True
23. True

24. a.  red, blue, yellow
25. c.  springiness
26. a.  vinyl
27. c.  proportion
28. b.  pinch-pleat
29. c.  Excavation of Pompeii
30. b.  pine, cedar, redwood
31. c.  artwork
32. a.  wool
33. c.  appliqué
34. b.  better quality of furniture
35. a.  makes a room look larger
36. b.  makes a room look smaller
37. a.  makes a room look larger
38. d.  progression of tints and shades of color
39. f.  focal point
40. c.  makes a room look shorter
41. a.  makes a room look larger
42. b.  makes a room look smaller
43. e.  reflect light

**Alternate Test Key**

1. c. staggering the invitation hours
2. c. a baby shower is usually given about a month before the baby is due
3. c. 30 minutes
4. a. lingerie
5. c. Offer to help May be seated.
6. a. Remove the fishbone with her thumb and forefinger.
7. b. The hostess unfolds her napkin.
8. a. Offer his seat mate a magazine or book.
9. b. Call Anna and honestly explain his money situation and ask her if she would want to go with him Dutch treat.
10. b. Use the plunger
11. a. Shut off the main source of water
12. False
13. False
14. True
15. False
16. False
17. False
18. False
19. True
20. False
21. False
22. True
23. True
24. True
25. True
26. False
27. True
28. True
29. True
30. True
31. Our generous, warm spirit, administering comfort and concern for others is a mirror reflecting the image of Christ in our character.

**Alternate Test Key**

1.  True
2.  True
3.  True
4.  True
5.  partly
6.  combination forms
7.  record book
8.  pension
9.  W-4 form
10. True
11. 50%
12. True
13. True
14. True
15. liable
16. True
17. True
18. verifying
19. True
20. True

**Alternate Test Key**

1. True
2. True
3. False
4. True
5. False
6. False
7. True
8. False
9. True
10. False
11. True
12. True
13. True
14. True
15. True
16. True
17. False
18. True
19. True
20. True
21. Answers may vary. The three-year old is starting to be interested in hearing with others. Sharing is an act of kindness and could and should be praised. Teaching Bible stories about kindness and helpfulness would be good.
22. Answers may vary. The two-year old is starting to observe adults and others, but not yet ready to participate. The best way to teach the two-year old to pray is through example.
23. Definitions may vary some, but age groups need to be as given in answer key.
    a. solitary play - the child plays alone; he is interested in his own activities, his own toys (1-2 or toddler)
    b. imaginative play - dramatic play-dressing up in clothes, "let's pretend" (3-4 or preschool)
    c. parallel play - the child plays next to another child, but not with him, children may be doing the same activity, for example, blocks (1-2 or toddler)
    d. cooperative play - the child can cooperate and play with one or more children, sharing and taking turns (4 or young school age)
24. Adult check: answers will vary. Be sure they include information from all four areas of development: physical, social, intellectual and spiritual.

**Alternate Test Key**

1. Answer may vary slightly.
   Relationship is the state of being related by kindred, affinity, or other alliances.

2. Answer may vary slightly.
   A friend is a person attached to another by feelings of affection or personal regard.

3. True

4. True

5. False, but you and they can learn from this mentoring technique.

6. True

7. False

8. True

9. True

10. True

11. True

12. True

13. True

14. False

15. False

16. True

17. Any order: glorify God, minister to others

18. Any order: doctrine, evangelizes

19. organization, cooperation

20. Answers will vary. Use the chart on page 45 of the text to help you grade this question.